M[illegible]
READY
THAN YOU THINK

Stepping into **your calling** as
a witness for Christ.

Frans Olivier

ISBN: 978-1-0681579-8-1

eISBN; 978-1-0681579-9-8

First published in 2025

Edited by jennhill.edits@gmail.com

Cover design by studioone9.online

Layout by Boutique Books

WHAT OTHERS HAVE SAID

I have known Frans Olivier for nearly 30 years and in that time I have found him to be insightful, humble and wise. But most of all he loves Jesus and is brilliantly gifted in sharing the good news with others. I recommend this book but more than that I commend the man who wrote it. He is a person worth listening to and learning from especially when it comes to sharing faith, stepping out in evangelism and seeing God move.

Dr Amy Orr-Ewing, Public Theologian, Honorary Lecturer University of Aberdeen, Distinguished Scholar Wheaton College.

Pastor Frans Olivier is passionate about bringing the gospel to the lost, but he takes missional work even further. He tirelessly ministers across Europe and the world to equip the next generation in evangelism and apologetics. He believes we must bring people to a saving faith and help them grow and mature, obeying Christ's command to make disciples throughout the earth. By imparting sound biblical doctrine through discipleship to future leaders, he ensures they are equipped to continue bringing the gospel to their campuses and communities and that each new believer can, in turn, disciple others.

Steve Murrell, President of Every Nation Churches & Ministries, Professor, Every Nation Seminary

I first met Frans as a student, when he was the campus pastor at my university in Cape Town. Now almost twenty years later, we are co-labourers for the gospel in London and Europe. Virtually every time we meet, I hear a new story about someone he has shared the gospel with. Over the years, I've also learned that if I hang around with him long enough, I too will inevitably end up in a gospel conversation with a stranger! Frans lives this authentically. This book makes the usually-intimidating idea of evangelism feel really simple and doable, and is filled with stories and illustrations which will give you confidence to share the gospel with fresh faith!

David Daniel, Lead Pastor of Every Nation London

Packed with powerful insights and inspiring stories of creative and faithful witness, Frans Olivier prepares and equips the spiritually barefoot believer with gospel running shoes! From the heart and pen of a proven evangelist, this fresh new book challenges and equips God's people to see gospel opportunities all around. He ties our laces for us with clarity and conviction and sends us on our way.

Rev. Dr. Joseph Boot, Founder and President of the Ezra Institute.

I have known Frans Olivier for close to forty years!! His passion to reach people with the love of Jesus burns just as brightly in person as it does in these pages. Frans is an evangelist with the heart and ability to share his gift with the body of Christ in practical and easy to follow ways. I recommend this book wholeheartedly – a powerful tool for this generation's pursuit of God's Great Commission.

Brenton Brown, Award–winning Christian artist and song writer

Filled with encouragement and practical steps, this book reminds us we don't need more qualifications–we are more ready than we realise! My good friend Frans Olivier lives a contagious Christianity. Soak in these pages, and you'll catch his passion for our most urgent assignment: to share the gospel with a waiting world.

Wayne Sandeman, Author of Revival Rain and lead pastor of Christian Life Church, Camps Bay, South Africa.

In *More Ready Than You Think* Frans offers a simple, but profound, resource that gently helps us overcome our lack of will in sharing our faith and helpfully builds our skill. All wrapped around with a host of examples both from the scriptures and from Frans' own experiences. Read it and take it seriously – it will help you introduce your friends to Jesus!

Myles Wilson, Northern Ireland, Mission advisor and a reluctant evangelist.

I first met Frans a few years back at an Evangelist Conference in England. Over lunch, we shared our passions for evangelism, equipping the church and the need for robust training.

The conversation was filled with enthusiasm and affirmations; 'exactly', 'amen', '100%', 'have you read...'. He shared with me his desire to write this book, and it is everything I expected and more. As I read it, my mind was filled with those same words of affirmation. I felt like I was reading it with Frans – a friend, a pastor, and a fellow evangelist. Frans has got the mix just right between scripture, stories, methodology, practical helps and sharing his challenges and vulnerability.

This is one of the most important books in evangelism I have ever read. When we kick off our next School of Evangelism in Belfast, every student will receive a copy of this book – it's that good.

Mitch, Co-founder and evangelist with Crown Jesus Ministries.

If you're ready to start sharing the gospel, this book is pure dynamite. It breaks inertia, fires you up, and gives you practical handles you can use right away. Frans combines fresh insight with tried-and-tested wisdom that really works. Read it. Do it. Keep at it. You'll soon see lives changed and more people coming to Jesus.

Themba Malaba, Director of Evangelism – Every Nation Southern Africa, Founder of Leading Evangelism

More Ready Than You Think is both inspiring and equipping. Frans draws from years of ministry and a deep passion for the gospel to encourage believers that "the Jesus you know is the Jesus you are ready to share". This book is a valuable tool for pastors, leaders, and churches committed to the Great Commission.

Gilbert Foliente, Bishop, Victory Metro Manila, Philippines

The harvest is ready. But is the church? Every Christian needs to know what the Gospel is, how to communicate it well, and be willing to actually go out and do it– not because we have to go, but because we are so filled with the love of God that we can't not go. More Ready Than You Think will get you there.

Aoife Keegan, Local Campus Minister, Dublin,
Campus Director for Every Nation Europe

This is a carefully crafted and prayerfully 'thought-out book. Frans gives a clear, compelling and compassionate motivation for why I share my faith, and practical and confidence building instruction for how I share my faith. The harvest is indeed plentiful and I now feel better equipped to play my part.

Rich Wilson, Fusion Movement leader

DEDICATION

To Rice Broocks, Floyd McClung and Wolfgang Eckleben who've each had a profound impact on my life.

I would like to express my heartfelt gratitude to my incredible wife, Deb, whose steadfast love, unwavering support and continuous belief in me have been invaluable throughout this journey. Her encouragement ensured that I persisted and completed this book. Lastly to my three children – Titus, Ethan and Ruth who've had a front row seat and been on the journey of taking the gospel to the nations with Deb and me.

CONTENTS

FOREWORD

I know of no one more ready to share the Gospel with others than Frans Olivier. From our first meeting in London many years ago, he has been singularly focused on sharing the good news with others and helping others do the same. This book will help anyone who cares about the same things. As an evangelist, he carries a fervent faith that is contagious. When you get the chance to be around someone like this you are forever changed. You can't go back to a life that ignores the urgency of the cause of Christ.

Several years ago, he preached a message that is now the title of the book you hold in your hands, *More Ready Than You Think*. This embodies the faith he carries for every believer to realise they don't have to wait to share the Gospel with others. The fear of *not* knowing enough keeps us from simply sharing what we *do* know. If you believe that Jesus is the Son of God and that He died on the cross and rose from the dead three days later then you carry the essence of the message needed to be communicated to every person on the planet. Sharing what you know is the beginning of the greatest adventure imaginable – participating in what's been called 'the Great Commission'.

In this book, Frans will take you through the steps of preparation and activation that will help you grow in your confidence and your fruitfulness. Following Christ is a lifelong journey...so is the calling to help others follow

Christ. As you persevere in being a witness you will be able to answer the questions that unbelievers struggle with and face the obstacles thrown in your way because of the spiritual opposition that comes with this great endeavour of telling others about the gift of salvation.

There are lots of approaches and programs people utilize to share with others; the most important thing that matters is whether there is lasting fruit that is produced. Frans has enormous credibility because of his global impact over many decades in helping people of all ages become fruitful in evangelism. The things he presents in this book will help anyone who is a sincere follower of Christ.

On a personal level, Frans has been a close friend and confidant in ministry. His integrity and sincerity make him an excellent addition to any ministry team. He can help anyone wanting to break out of the disappointment that marks so many well-meaning evangelistic endeavours. He can help identify and train other evangelists who can continue the ministry efforts that are launched.

It makes me extremely happy to see this book, *More Ready Than You Think* in print. I know how much it will help those who read and put these strategies into practice. If nothing else, there will be things you carry away from this project that you can incorporate into your own existing strategy. Frans has done this with things I have written and taught. He has taken the time to bring us this important work that combines some of the best practices of evangelists and ministry leaders from around the world.

As you survey churches around the world you will find a common need for help in training believers to reach unbelievers. The statistics give a grim picture of how few are effective in doing this. Frans has taken the time to shine the light in the darkness and to help us turn things around in this critical hour of human history. May the Lord lift you into a new level of faith to reach further than you ever thought possible.

Dr. Rice Broocks
Co-founder Every Nation Churches and Ministries
Best-selling author of *God's Not Dead*

PREFACE

'There are two reasons today why people are not yet Christians. One, they've never met a Christian. Two, they have met a Christian.'[1]

This insight from prominent UK evangelist, J. John, is so true. Ultimately, I wrote *More Ready than You Think* to help 'not-yet-Christians' meet Christians, and when they do, to discover good reasons to become one.

The idea to write this book originated in 2012 after I spoke at an evangelism conference in Nashville, USA. Following my presentation, globally-recognised evangelist Dr Rice Broocks, approached me and suggested that the message I had delivered should be turned into a book. Two weeks later, at a church leaders' conference in Cape Town, South Africa, the missionary Floyd McClung (who like Dr Broocks is also a best-selling author), made the same recommendation after my talk. Receiving this advice from two well-established figures in the field prompted me to consider their suggestion seriously. The topic I discussed at both events was titled: *More Ready Than You Think*, which encouraged individuals to share their beliefs about Jesus Christ in everyday conversations. The message aimed to inspire outreach and positive engagement with others.

My hope is the stories will inspire you, the principles will guide you, the Word of God will inform you and the insights will activate you. We have good news worth sharing. The world needs to know. Sometimes people are more willing to hear than we are willing to share.

I have participated in evangelism initiatives that have created a sense of obligation and effort, which is intimidating and overwhelming. The good news we get to share is too good to do it this way, and I don't think this is how Jesus wants us to seek and save those who are lost. While Jesus did send His disciples out as 'sheep among wolves', we can see that there was joy in the journey!

I was greatly encouraged when Jenni, my editor and writing coach, told me that the impact she felt while editing my book encouraged her to guide someone towards faith! She will tell you that she is not an evangelist. I took that as an indicator that God's grace rests on this message.

More Ready Than You Think is designed to invite readers to engage in a purposeful, joy-filled journey with Jesus as part of His mission.

As with any significant undertaking, thorough preparation is essential. During our family's recent visit to Beijing, we learnt that the Forbidden City took fifteen years to construct. Our guide told us that ten of those years were devoted exclusively to preparation – sourcing materials and readying the foundation – while the actual building process occupied the remaining five years. This book will assist you in thorough preparation, and in building a solid foundation for making a meaningful impact through the gospel.

It is not a comprehensive guide on evangelism. While apologetics – preparing to explain and defend your beliefs – is valuable, it is not the focus here, and neither do I comprehensively address the topic of spirit-empowered evangelism, although I do place significant importance on it. Another area I don't cover in this book, is that of social responsibility, though I acknowledge it as essential to fulfilling community and spiritual objectives. I encourage you to seek out other resources on these topics.

I have kept things simple and centred on building your confidence and skills, to sharing faith through conversation. My hope is that you can build on these foundations as you explore and discover effective ways to build bridges and break barriers for ministering the gospel.

I trust that you will be encouraged by the accounts of ordinary men and women who, in finding courage in God to step out in faith, have seen the impact of the gospel. (In certain stories, I have changed their names to preserve anonymity.)

My prayer is that you will make two profound discoveries as you read: one, the harvest of lost souls is more ready than you think; and two, you are more ready than you think to respond to the ready harvest around you.

Frans Olivier

INTRODUCTION

PUTTING ON YOUR SHOES OF READINESS

My shoes were brand new! How on earth had the shoeshine guy convinced me they needed a polish?

I was in the bustling Johannesburg airport, with people young and old rushing to get to their boarding gates. Bumping, jostling, some were casually window shopping, while others stared at the elevated screens, checking their flight status. And there I was sitting in the shoeshine chair. He had stopped me just as I made it through security. Smartly dressed all in black, with a big beaming smile, he was both enthusiastic and persistent.

'Sir, let me shine your shoes. I'll make them good.'

'No, thank you; besides, I don't have any cash.' I responded politely, fully expecting the conversation to end there. After all, I needed to find my boarding gate for the connecting flight to Cape Town. I was hoping to squeeze in that desperately needed coffee after my twelve-hour flight from London.

'Not to worry, sir. Let me shine them. I promise I'll make them really good.'

'Honestly, I don't have any cash on me, and they are only trainers!'

'Sir, look here see this scuff mark,' he said pointing to a grey smudge on the shiny white sole of my right shoe. 'Let me make it good for you, don't worry about the money' he persisted, still with his big beaming smile.

I gave in. His enthusiastic persistence broke through my resolve, and I traded that coffee for a shoeshine I didn't really need. As I sat down it dawned on me that it was only yesterday that I had bought this pair of shoes, yet somehow this guy, Mr Enthusiasm, had persuaded me into a shoeshine.

His friend joined us and to my surprise began polishing my canvas bag. I was about to object but then thought better of it. I was curious. I started asking questions about their lives. Effortlessly and naturally, the conversation steered towards their beliefs about God. Mr Enthusiasm seemed distracted, clearly thinking about the next customer he could persuade to his throne-like shoe-shining chair. But Mr Bag Polisher became quietly vulnerable as he shared his struggle with alcohol, and how he'd like to believe in God but thought God wouldn't be interested in someone like him.

I asked if anyone had ever explained to them who God is and what He's done for us. Mr Bag Polisher shook his head.

'Would you like me to?'

With both responding with a firm yes, I briefly explained the good news of Jesus: what He's done for us, and our need to be saved from our sin. I shared the vision of God's glorious Kingdom. I outlined one or two key Bible passages and clarified the critical eternal choice we all need to make. Finally, I offered the opportunity for them to pray and accept Jesus' glorious gift of eternal life.

Mr Enthusiasm politely declined and headed off in pursuit of another customer. But Mr Bag Polisher was curious, though not yet persuaded. He said he was not ready, but asked if we could keep in touch. I gave him a gospel tract and we exchanged contact details.

At 4:14 a.m. the next morning I received this message on my phone: ‘Morning Frans...it’s me from airport the shoe-cleaning guy...I will like to take the journey with you to know Jesus.’

*

What started as a reluctant travel-weary conversation, ended in two precious people hearing the good news of Jesus, and one of them making a decision of eternal consequence.

How ready do you feel to have a conversation like this?

I want to propose, that if you don’t feel very ready, with God, you are more ready than you think. Whether you feel ready or not, the harvest of lost souls, like the two shoeshine guys, is more ready than you may think (John 4:35). There are people all around us, ready to journey towards Jesus, or even ready to commit their lives to Him. Jesus is inviting us to join Him on a journey to seek and save those who are lost.

What shoes do you own? Whether you have many or few, every pair of shoes you have is designed for a purpose. If they’re for football, they will look very different to a pair of high heels or smart leather shoes for the office.

In Ephesians 6, the apostle Paul writes to a group of believers in the city of Ephesus, encouraging them to put on the full armour of God. He talks about weapons – for fighting God’s enemy the devil – and defensive gear, such as shields, breastplates and helmets. It’s all to help us stand strong and advance God’s glorious Kingdom; but here’s what he has to say about shoes: *‘And, as shoes for your feet, having put on the readiness given by the gospel of peace'* (Ephesians 6:15 ESV).

Interesting. The gospel is associated with shoes, not protective armour, or swords and belts, but *shoes*. And notice there is also mention of *readiness*. But why shoes? Shoes make you mobile. They are used for walking or running, or to enhance an activity.

There are two insights I'd love for you to take away from this introduction and keep them in mind while reading through the pages of this book.

1. The gospel needs to be mobile.
2. Readiness is something you put on.

1. THE GOSPEL NEEDS TO BE MOBILE

The apostle Paul writing to believers in Rome stated: *'How beautiful are the feet of those who bring good news!'* (Romans 10:15). Did you spot the connection? Feet and good news! Feet need shoes of readiness to take the good news where it needs to go. But interestingly, before that in verse 14, Paul points out that people will not know the good news unless they hear it. Isn't that stating the obvious? He adds, how will they hear unless someone tells them? While it is obvious, it's something we may not be conscious of unless it is pointed out to us. But hopefully when we realise just how incredible and life-changing the news is, and that people need to hear it to respond to it, we will embrace our role as proclaimers of this glorious good news!

When I was a student, I heard a preacher talk about farmers who cover wells in desert regions so that others can't get to them. A person can die of thirst right on top of a hidden well, not knowing there is water within reach. There are people dying without the gospel because we have blocked our wells. We have living waters within us, but they need to flow like a river. How will they know unless we go?

We need to find those shoes, designed for taking the good news of salvation and restoration to people and places ready to receive it.

2. READINESS IS SOMETHING WE PUT ON

What makes us ready for something? Readiness to tackle certain things often takes planning and preparation; it might even require training if a particular skill is needed. According to the Cambridge online dictionary 'readiness' is defined as 'willingness or a state of being prepared for something'.

Preparation and willingness! When it comes to sharing your faith, how prepared do you feel? How willing are you?

The apostle Paul seemed to think that readiness, like a pair of shoes, is something you put on. If God was not part of the equation, then that would make no sense: you need specialised training to be ready. How can you simply 'put it on'?

God can empower you supernaturally to be His witness beyond your own immediate competency! Acts 1:8 says that when the Spirit comes upon you, you will receive power to be His witness. He also promises to give you the words when you don't know what to say. With God's presence and your shoes of readiness, you are ready enough to step into your calling as a witness for Christ and to bring lost people into His Kingdom and help them as they join His family. And with God on the journey with you, you will grow as you go!

YOUR READINESS, THE MESSAGE, AND A METHOD

As I had the joy and privilege of sharing my faith with the shoeshine guys, my prayer for you is to have similar opportunities, and to have the confidence and competence to grab them boldly. I'm hoping my book will help you; it's structured into three distinct parts: Preparation, Communication, and Activation.

PREPARATION

Preparation involves cultivating our willingness to share our faith. By abiding in His love and presence, and through the revelation that we are *made* to fish, we are compelled by His compassion to be witnesses and ambassadors of our heavenly King. If not-yet-Christians are to become Christians through our witness, we need to represent the message well.

COMMUNICATION

At the core of our message is the death, burial, and resurrection of Jesus. Through His sacrifice, God provided a way to renew His creation. It is essential that this message is clear and meaningful to us personally, and we must be fully convinced of its truth and relevance for ourselves and those around us. Understanding and internalising the profound impact and significance of our beliefs, equips us with greater confidence and competence to communicate them effectively. As we clarify the substance of our message and appreciate its importance, our ability to communicate it will be strengthened.

ACTIVATION

Where do we start with sharing our faith? How do we start and steer conversations for sharing the good news of Jesus Christ? What do we do if someone wants to commit their lives to Christ? Here, I share a simple, three-step plan for putting on your shoes to get going with getting the good news out on time.

*

I wish I could tell you that my shoes of readiness are always on my feet as they should be. But unfortunately, they are not. For two years, I had been praying for my neighbour, Trevor. Then one day, my wife Deb called out to me while I was working busily on something that seemed very important at the time. She pointed out that an ambulance was parked outside, and Trevor was waving goodbye to some of our other neighbours as he was wheeled towards it. She suggested I go and greet him and possibly pray for him. I considered it briefly but was too absorbed in what I was doing. I thought I would pay him a visit when he got back from hospital. About two days later we heard he had passed away. My heart broke. I'd had such a deep burden for him and desired to have the opportunity for a gospel conversation. But, distracted by my busyness, the opportunity was lost. To this day, I don't know if Trevor went to be with Jesus or went to a Christless eternity; there were no indicators that he'd made a commitment to follow Christ. On that day, I did not put on the shoes of readiness that come from the gospel of peace. It's a moment I can never get back. I will never know because I did not go. A person's lifespan is their only window of opportunity to make an eternal decision to be a member of God's family and a citizen of His Kingdom.

I never want another Trevor moment. I hope you don't have one either. If you have already then receive God's grace to release you of any sense of guilt or condemnation. Instead, let the memory of that person and that moment motivate you to raise your readiness for the next opportunity.

Consider people, or places where your shoes of readiness can take you. Think of someone right now who isn't yet saved. Picture them. Pray for them. God loves that person more than you can possibly imagine. He values them so much that He paid the ultimate price for them; He sacrificed His own life to save theirs.

Carl F.H. Henry, one of the founders of Fuller Seminary in California, and profound theological thought leader made this statement: 'The gospel is only good news if it gets there in time.' [1]

Think about that for a moment. There's no question that we have good news for a world broken and devastated by the destructive evil of sin. Glorious image bearers of God are broken, bankrupt, thirsty souls in desperate need of the living waters Jesus offers. But time is of the essence; it's very *bad* news if an unsaved person dies and hasn't heard the good news. I will never know this side of eternity if the gospel reached Trevor *in time*; there's the possibility that it did not.

Will you join me in putting on the shoes of readiness, cultivating your willingness and raising your readiness? Let's join Jesus in the adventurous journey of getting the good news of the gospel where it needs to go and getting it there on time. Together, let's avoid lost opportunities and trust God for many 'shoeshine guy encounters.'

You are more ready than you think!

SECTION ONE

PREPARATION

YOUR NOTES

CHAPTER ONE

RAISING YOUR READINESS

Imperial College, London, is home to the brightest and best in fields of science, engineering and medicine. We were doing an outreach, and on this particular occasion, a former student and friend, Ann-Marie, was part of the team. She was having an intense conversation with a Muslim. He was bright and prepared, and he asked her questions she couldn't answer. Frustrated and overwhelmed, she walked away discouraged.

Instead of giving up, she devoured *Seeking Allah, Finding Jesus* by Nabeel Qureshi, because her heart burned with desire to see Muslims find Jesus, and she wanted to be ready for another encounter next time she met one.

She was presented with another opportunity when an Iranian joined the Alpha Course (a course exploring the Christian faith) she and her husband Paul were running in their home. After weeks of prayer, and them answering many of his sincere questions, he discovered the Jesus the Quran hadn't told him about. This precious Muslim prayed with her and Paul, and received Jesus.

Initially, Ann-Marie wasn't ready to reach Muslims, but she was willing and intentional to raise her readiness to do so.

In this section, you will discover how to raise your readiness by cultivating your willingness. God can do more through someone willing and untrained than someone trained and unwilling. But imagine what God can do through someone both willing, and trained! Willingness is a vital ingredient that triggers activation.

James puts it this way: *'Do not merely listen to the word, and so deceive yourselves. Do what it says'* (James 1:22). Doing what it says requires an act of your will. Did you get that? An act of your *will*! The state of your will determines your willingness.

The Oxford Dictionary defines willingness as the quality of being happy and ready to do something. It emphasises a person's readiness to engage in an action when needed.

My prayer for you is that like Ann-Marie, you will push through the barriers and discouragements with resilience, because of your willingness. Let's look at how to cultivate it!

THE UNTRAINED NON-PROFESSIONAL

In the scorching noonday Samaria sun, Jesus (God-in-the-flesh) is tired, hungry and needing a rest. He sends his disciples to the town to get food while He takes a break at a well. He's in his thirties and on his own, when a woman with a colourful history, and from an opposing culture, saunters past.

I am referring to Jesus' encounter with the woman outside the Samaritan town of Sychar. This happened in the early part of Jesus' three-year ministry. He had selected His core team of twelve disciples and He was teaching and modelling the ways of the Kingdom He was proclaiming. He was investing in their readiness to share the same message.

At the time of his encounter with the woman, there was hostility and distrust between Jews and Samaritans. When Jesus asks her for a drink, her response is very telling: *'You are a Jew, and I am a Samaritan woman. How can you ask me for a drink?'* (John 4:9).

Clearly Jesus was breaking from acceptable cultural norms. One could surmise that He was desperately thirsty and was willing to waiver acceptable norms in His desire for a drink. But His response to her question would suggest otherwise: *'If you knew the gift of God and who it is that asks you for a drink, you would have asked him and he would have given you living water... Indeed, the water I give them will become in them a spring of water welling up to eternal life'* (John 4:10,14).

Instead of explaining Himself and repeating His request, He offers God's gift of eternal life. She was ready.

When the disciples return, this shamed woman, armed with only her testimony, proclaims the good news of Jesus to people who know her messy history (during their discourse Jesus reveals she has had five husbands and the man she is now with is not her husband). The result? Jesus delays his plans, stays two days, and an orphaned town receives the message of the promised Kingdom.

Would one expect a woman with such a colourful past and such a fresh encounter with Jesus to impact a whole town for Christ?

Sandwiched between the woman's encounter and the town's response, Jesus has a moment with His disciples. *'Don't you have a saying, "It's still four months until harvest"? I tell you, open your eyes and look at the fields! They are ripe for harvest'* (John 4:35).

Think about it. A team of trained professionals go into a very ripe harvest and they have no impact. In stark contrast, the shamed non-professional, armed with only her testimony, brings a whole town to Christ. The gentle rebuke is clear: the harvest is more ready than they think, and the implication is they should be too. Why did the woman have impact, and the disciples not? Can we learn from the woman's readiness? My observation is that the woman had the following:

1. An encounter with Jesus.
2. A willingness to share.
3. An opportunity to proclaim.

Have you had an encounter with Jesus? I hope so. Are you willing to share your faith? If your answer is no, I hope you can at least say, 'not yet,' and with God's help be willing to be willing. Are there opportunities for you to proclaim? Perhaps you feel like the answer is *no*, but maybe, like Jesus said, the harvest around you is more ready than you think?

1. AN ENCOUNTER WITH JESUS

Andy and I were eleven years old, kneeling on the prickly grass, facing each other. His eyebrows were knit together and his nose wrinkled. The creases at the corners of his eyes indicated the intensity with which he wanted to pray. At the worst possible moment, Andy's mum appeared at the kitchen door. Despite the hot African sun beating down on us it felt like a bucket of cold water had just been dumped on me.

'Andy, time to go!'

'Will she be angry with me when she finds out Andy wants to commit his life to Jesus?' I thought. I hadn't even asked for it. He was the one who had started asking questions about God. In my mind I began building my defence.

'Andy, it's okay, we can pray another day. You need to go.'

With eyes tightly shut, he waved his hand wildly as if shooing away a fly, and shouted back, 'Go away, mother, I need to pray!'

And then turning to me he said, 'Let's pray!'

Unsure of myself, I reluctantly led him in a prayer. When he finally opened his eyes, I saw that he was changed. I could see in his eyes what I had felt when my mum had prayed the same prayer with me a few years previously.

*

Despite my reluctance and lack of confidence, Andy experienced what it means to be saved that day. I had no training to share the good news of Jesus. I had not even initiated the conversation, and I certainly did not feel ready to lead him to make the most important decision of his life. Yet, despite me not feeling ready I was more ready than I thought.

What I did have, was an encounter with Jesus. When I was five-years old, sitting in a car with my mum, I asked questions about God and what it meant to be a Christian. She shared the good news of Jesus and my need to be saved from sin. It made sense, and that day I committed my life to Christ.

When you are in a relationship with Him, you can introduce Him to someone else. The Jesus you know is the Jesus you are ready to share. That is our starting point.

I knew enough so that my readiness to share could collide with Andy's readiness to respond. Like Jesus told the disciples in John 4:35, He knew that Andy's readiness was not 'four months' away, but like the harvest, he was ready then.

It takes faith to share our faith. We can't give what we have not received. But once we've received it, we have it for others to receive from us.

The woman at the well had an encounter with Jesus that triggered her to tell others about what He had done. This was good news. Clearly her life was radically impacted. She found hope, meaning and contentment. The deepest needs of her soul were met. If coming to faith is just about receiving religious information, it would not trigger that kind of response. Her heart was impacted, her mind was informed, and she was motivated with a willingness to tell others.

Our faith is not a religious claim but a relationship with almighty God, the creator of the universe. Is God someone or something you just know about, like a celebrity you follow on social media? I hope not. My hope is that you have experienced intimacy with God, the joy of walking in relationship with Him. When we share our faith with someone, we want to introduce Jesus as a friend and not as a historical figure. When we meet Jesus, and receive Him, He becomes many things to us: Lord, saviour, healer, teacher, friend, shepherd, provider, and the list goes on. Ultimately, we are in relationship with Him because we decided to put our trust in Him.

Elsewhere we will address how to raise our readiness beyond the starting point of being in relationship with Jesus. When I shared with Andy, all I had was my own testimony and the Holy Spirit guiding me. Like the woman at the well, I had met Jesus and all I had was a story to tell. But like her, that made me ready enough. You already have that too. For now, that is enough to know that you are ready to share the good news of Jesus.

2. A WILLINGNESS TO SHARE

You may be ready, but if you are not willing, you will not share your faith. If you are reading this book, it indicates that something in you wants to be fruitful in helping others find Jesus. I believe that there is a willingness already in you. Perhaps you are regularly sharing the good news of Jesus with fruitfulness, or perhaps like me you struggle at times to do it consistently. Or perhaps you've never shared your faith with anyone, or you've tried and had a catastrophic experience.

When the disciples were in Sychar why did they not tell people about Jesus? Were they too busy? After all, Jesus sent them to get food. Perhaps they were too preoccupied with getting food to be concerned about introducing people to Jesus. Were they too tired? Perhaps. Were they intimidated? There was animosity between Jews and Samaritans after all, and they were outnumbered. Were they indifferent? That's a definite possibility. There are many possible reasons that could have affected their willingness to tell anyone about Jesus. There are many things that can also affect our willingness.

In the Gospel of Matthew, when Jesus sent His disciples out for the first time to proclaim the good news of the Kingdom, He instructed them not to go to the towns of the Samaritans (Matthew 10:5). Sychar would have been one of them. That is strange. Why would He do that? In contrast, in Acts 1:8 when Jesus was wrapping up His season of incarnational ministry, He instructed the same disciples and others to go to Samaria. Sychar would have been included. What changed?

Years ago, I heard a preacher reflect on this contrast. His conclusion? The disciples, despite being trained by the best teacher one could hope for, were not yet ready in Matthew 10, because of their prejudice towards Samaritans. We don't know for certain if that is the case but what is evident is that on that day in Sychar they did not tell anyone about Jesus. By spending time with Jesus their willingness towards Samaritans changed. Our willingness can change too.

What do you do when you are ready but struggling to be willing? I think that's exactly what Jesus addressed in His instructions to His disciples: *'...I tell you, lift up your eyes and look...' (John 4:35).*

Something happens when we see people. I mean really see them; when we take our eyes off ourselves and our own needs and demands, and there are many, and instead we consider the needs and demands of others, especially their need for Jesus. Often, as I pray for people who don't know Jesus and I think about their lives without the love, joy, peace, contentment, and comfort that I get to enjoy through relationship with God, I find that my willingness to share increases.

3. OPPORTUNITIES TO PROCLAIM

Five million: this is how many people travel on a London bus every day.[1] Not every month or every year, but *every day*. Jesus loves and cares for every single last one of them. He knows their most intimate details, their struggles, pains, delights and passions. He knows them and He loves them.

One of those five million is Enid. In April 2019, the mundane and bothersome space of an often-crowded London bus became a place of harvest readiness. Enid was attending the course on conversational evangelism that my wife, Deb, and I had developed. During one of the training sessions, she closed her eyes and asked God to show her people or places for an intentional spiritual conversation. Suddenly a face came to mind: a person she occasionally saw on the bus. She'd only had brief, but polite conversations with her. She prayed for courage and asked God for an opportunity to invite her for a coffee.

The following week at the evangelism training, Enid was bursting with excitement as she shared the following: 'I saw the lady the very next day and we agreed to meet for coffee. In the coffee shop, with tears in her eyes, she repented and gave her heart to Jesus.'

One of those five million people encountered Jesus and came to faith because Enid lifted her eyes and looked at the harvest. She was willing to pursue an opportunity God gave her when she prayed.

I make it a practice when going about my daily activities – sitting in a coffee shop, walking down the street, travelling on public transport – to consciously look at the people around me. Often, I take a moment to pray for them. I consider the fact that God knows every single one of them. He loves them and cares about the details of their lives. I ask God to give me a love for them like He has. I ask Him for the courage I need to initiate a conversation.

I also pray for people I know who don't yet know Jesus: neighbours, family, friends, and acquaintances. I ask God to show me needs in their lives and how I can serve them, how I can be a blessing to them. I pray that God may soften their hearts to the gospel. I ask God for opportunities to share the good news of Jesus with them.

CONCLUSION: RAISING YOUR READINESS

All of us have a harvest we are ready for. All of us have future harvests we can prepare for. They may not be on a London bus, or a curious Muslim, but there are people and places available to everyone of us.

The Samaritan woman was ready for her harvest. The disciples needed a journey with Jesus to root out their prejudice. Ann-Marie needed to learn from the articulate and persuasive former Muslim, Nabeel Qureshi. Enid needed a moment to lift her eyes to see the harvest that was ready around her.

In this book we will look at what we can do to raise the readiness of those not yet ready to respond to Jesus. We will also look at how we can discern between ready harvest and harvest that is not yet ready. We will learn how to raise our own readiness to share our faith.

For now, we acknowledge that not everyone is ready for Jesus, and our aim is to seek people whose readiness to respond can collide with our readiness to share.

If you have had an *encounter* with Jesus, if you are *willing* to share and if you see *opportunities* to proclaim, then, you are ready enough! Say: 'Yes Lord, here I am, send me!'

You are now more ready than you think!

CHAPTER TWO

WILLINGNESS FROM ABIDING

It took every bit of self-control I possessed not to exceed the speed limit. All I could think about was not being late. My thoughts were interrupted by the high-pitched voice of my four-year-old son in the back seat: 'Dad, I need sweets!'

Trying not to show my slight irritation at this interruption I responded: 'Titus, you don't *need* sweets, you *want* sweets.'

Thoughtful silence from the back seat. The little voice piped up again. 'But dad, then I want to *need* sweets.'

With such cleverness from such a young mind, how could I resist? Titus got the sweets he wanted, but didn't need.

*

What do you do when what you need is not what you want? Let's be honest, sharing our faith is not something we always want to do, but have you considered that it could be something we all need to do? How do you shift from not wanting to share your faith, to wanting to, and being willing to do it?

I am excited to tell you about something Jesus emphasised in John 15: the power of abiding in Him. When it comes to being a follower of Jesus, you have to start with *abiding* in Him before *doing* anything for Him. This includes sharing your faith.

Abide in me, and I in you. As the branch cannot bear fruit by itself, unless it abides in the vine, neither can you, unless you abide in me. I am the vine; you are the branches. Whoever abides in me and I in him, he it is that bears much fruit, for apart from me you can do nothing.

John 15:4-5 ESV

WHAT DOES IT MEAN TO ABIDE?

The word *abide* is a verb. It is more than just believing in Jesus; it means to have an active continuous relationship with Him. It has the same root as the word *abode,* which is a home. To abide, or remain in Jesus, is to become family with Him: to dwell, and do life together.

Jesus gave this instruction just hours before being arrested and nailed to the cross. He was calling His disciples into communion with Him. Despite what was about to happen to Him, He wanted them to remain in Him so that they could receive the nourishing life He would provide. Wonderful things happen when Jesus becomes more than an add on to your life. He uses the analogy of a branch connected to a vine, a picture of transferred nourishment as a source of life. When you are a branch connected to Him as a vine, His life flows in you and through you.

How can you abide in Him? Abiding means spending time with Jesus in worship and in prayer. It means studying His Word, the Bible, and allowing it to impact your life. Abiding means fellowshipping with other believers and experiencing God's love, His instruction, and even correction through being in community. Ultimately, abiding in Jesus is receiving His love, truth and transformational instruction in your life.

ABIDING PRODUCES FRUIT

Jesus also makes mention of fruit. His life flowing in you produces fruit others can receive from. It is the fruit that comes from abiding that can shift us to *want* what we need when it comes to sharing our faith. What fruit is Jesus talking about?

Close your eyes. Think about your favourite fruit. Picture it. Think back to a moment when you bit into that fruit and experienced the pleasure that the nourishing, sweet-tasting juicy flesh produced in you. Feel the texture and enjoy the memory of that delicious moment.

A moment that comes to my mind was on a missions trip when I was a student. To begin with, we had a gruelling three-day car journey negotiating many potholed roads between Cape Town and a small town in Zambia called Livingstone. So, there I was, travel weary, sleep deprived and having just preached my first sermon. I was nestled in a heavily-laden mango tree. I remember plucking one perfectly ripe golden mango after another, relishing every juicy bite dripping with refreshing goodness.

Fruit has a purpose. There is a reason Jesus talks about our fruitfulness through abiding. Fruits, in their very nature, are designed for two things:

1. It is designed to be enjoyed – the juicy flesh.
2. It is designed to reproduce – the seed.

The first purpose helps achieve the second – reproduction. The juicy, nourishing, delicious flesh of the fruit needs to be desirable to attract all kinds of potential consumers. It also contains seed that has the power to reproduce and eventually manifest more fruit for further reproduction.

FRUIT FOR THE BELIEVER

In John 15:9-10, 12-13 and 17, Jesus mentions the word *love.* He speaks about God's love for us, but also our love for others. In verse 11 Jesus speaks about joy. Love and joy are mentioned many times throughout scripture. In Galatians 5 they are referred to specifically as fruit. *'But the fruit of the Spirit is* ***love, joy,*** *peace, forbearance, kindness, goodness, faithfulness, gentleness, self-control; against such things there is no law'* (Galatians 5:22-23, my emphasis).

Notice it says, fruit of *the Spirit.* God's Holy Spirit was sent to us after Jesus ascended. It is His Spirit that flows to us, in us and through us, providing the nourishing life that comes from abiding.

Jesus, in John 15, and the apostle Paul in Galatians 5, are referring to godly characteristics that are intended for every believer. They are descriptive of God's very nature, His character. They are also descriptive of what we are called to be as His image bearers in this world.

Love and joy mentioned in John 15 are just two of the nine fruits mentioned in Galatians 5. All these are God's characteristics that form in us as we abide in Jesus, who is the vine. They are also descriptive of God's heavenly Kingdom, destined for earth.

Jesus instructed His followers to pray, *'your kingdom come, your will be done, on earth as it is in heaven'* (Matthew

6:10). God wants love, joy, peace, goodness, kindness etc. to prevail on earth. If we look at the world around us, these qualities are desperately needed. God's plan is that the Kingdom comes to us through our abiding in Him, and then flows through us to the world.

All the fruits of the Spirit, and the fruit Jesus spoke about, are potent for reproducing and advancing God's manifest Kingdom in lives, families, communities, cities, nations and ultimately in all of creation.

The presence of the Holy Spirit in our lives produces fruits of love, joy, peace, patience, kindness, goodness, faithfulness, gentleness and self-control. When manifest in our lives, these qualities and descriptions of His character and holy Kingdom, attract people to His reality.

Jesus said if you will remain in Him – abide in Him – then you will bear much fruit. Think about this: you become like the people you spend time with. Spend time with Jesus, and you will become like Jesus. Spending quality time with Him through abiding, produces His character, His manner, His way of thinking to shape who you are and what you become. The Father cultivates the way of His Kingdom through the presence of His Son and Holy Spirit in your life. He does this as you spend time in His presence.

Spending time with Jesus, and becoming like Jesus who loves and cares deeply for the lost, will transform your heart for the lost. Abiding in Jesus cultivates your willingness. It produces desire in you, with love and compassion, to want to engage the lost with the good news of Jesus.

The benefit of abiding is not limited to the life of a believer only. The fruit that is manifest in you, can also have impact on the lives of non-believers around you.

FRUIT FOR THE UNBELIEVER

We were doing covert outreach on a Chinese campus at a time when China was attempting to reintegrate into the global market. If we were reported, there could be consequences; it was risky, but the students needed the gospel. They were still living with the generational legacy of Chairman Mao Zedong, champion of communism, who had ruled China with an iron fist decades before.

Students had to learn English. Every campus had an 'English Corner': a place designated for practising the language, and foreigners were invited to get involved. Since we were reaching out to students, we didn't have to be asked twice.

When asked what they believed, the common answer was, 'I believe in myself.'

Drilled in through the education system, it is a statement that captures the bankrupt philosophy that God is not real, and ultimately we only have ourselves to rely on. Yet, living in an environment that sought to destroy all access to a spiritual life, their starvation had produced a hunger in many of them.

One student, who seemed especially eager to talk about spiritual things, asked Corné, my good friend and partner in the gospel, 'what is the hope I see in your eyes?'

The fruit of the Spirit in Corné's life drew this student, like a hungry deer, to a fruit-bearing tree. By the end of the week the student had shed the belief system that had

starved him for so long, and received Jesus, the Bread of Life; at last his hunger was satisfied.

We do not have to go to a spiritually-starved communist nation to have the same response. Ruth, who was also on this mission trip, works in the head office of a major department store in the UK. While she was doing our evangelism training, and practising the principles of abiding, one of her colleagues asked her, 'Ruth, I see such a peace in you, where does it come from?'

'You know,' she answered, 'I've not always been like this. Would you like a coffee sometime where I could share with you what happened?'

Again, another spiritually-starved person, drawn by the fruit manifested on a branch connected to the life-giving vine of Jesus. God in you glorifies God through you. As Jesus stated in John 15:8*:* 'This is to my Father's glory, that you bear much fruit, showing yourselves to be my disciples.'

As you become a loving person, the love of God in you affects the willingness of non-believers to explore Jesus. They become attracted to the love, the joy, the peace and other godly characteristics they see in you, and begin to desire the same fruit. The fruit of the Spirit produced in you has the potent power to catalyse desire for God's Kingdom in others, and offers the seed of His Kingdom that can be reproduced in them through the good news of the gospel.

That is why Jesus said that bearing fruit glorifies the Father and shows that we are His disciples. We look, sound and behave like Him when we abide in Him, and we become beacons of hope to a desperate and broken world.

CONCLUSION: CULTIVATING YOUR WILLINGNESS THROUGH ABIDING

Titus wanted what he did not need, and then acknowledged he wanted to need it. When it comes to sharing your faith, you can find yourself not wanting to do it. That is normal. How about making a start by *wanting* to want to do it?

Jesus spent time abiding. We read throughout the gospels how He would take time out from His busy schedule to prioritise time with His heavenly Father. He modelled powerful Kingdom living. If Jesus needed time to abide, how much more do we? By spending time with Jesus, He can impart His heart, and transform your heart to feel as He feels about the lost. Your unwillingness can shift to willingness when you abide in Him. In the process, His character is formed in you; you are transformed to become like Him. His love, joy, peace, goodness, kindness, and the other amazing qualities of Jesus and His Kingdom become manifest in your life.

You are made to be like God. You are made in His image. Every person you meet is also made to be like God. When they see the fruit of His character in you, it can awaken in them the awareness of who they are meant to be, but are not yet, and can open doors of opportunity for you to share with them the hope that is found in Jesus.

Raising your readiness by cultivating your willingness, starts with your personal relationship and intimacy with Jesus.

CHAPTER THREE

WILLINGNESS FROM BEING

The Eiffel Tower was not visible. In front of me were the seven arches of the university, set against the starry sky. It was as if they were taunting me, daring me even to set foot on the campus. The rest of the Paris outreach team was paired up, but I was alone.

Would tonight be different? I thought. There had been a subtle hostility, especially from the campus authorities who state in their constitution that no proselytising is allowed. I was trusting for conversations that would lead to sharing the good news of Jesus, but they had not yet materialised.

I fixed my attention on the creamy-coloured building beyond the arches – a social hub, now illuminated by golden light. I wanted that night to be different, so I prayed, *'Jesus, you said, "Follow me and I will* ***make you*** *a fisher of men", now please* ***make me*** *a fisher. How should I fish?'*

The response was immediate: 'Find an empty table and wait.'

I could not help but smile with anticipation as I proceeded to the chateau-like building with its dining hall heaving with hundreds of hungry students.

After grabbing a meal, and circling the hall several times to find an empty table, I sat down. Forty minutes passed, and with my meal now finished, I watched as students walked past me only to settle at the crowded tables next to mine.

It was puzzling. I prayed, 'Jesus, you gave me a clear instruction. I obeyed. What's going on?'

Then I heard it: a South African accent? I strained to listen. Sure enough, there it was again, two girls in animated conversation three tables away from me. I walked over to them.

'Hi, my name is Frans. Are either of you South African?'

One of the girls squealed with delight at meeting a fellow *Saffa* (slang for South African); her friend was from Mozambique. They invited me to sit down, and with keen interest I asked them about themselves. Their broad smiles told me they were enjoying connecting as much as I was.

Then I saw a picture, like in a dream, of a tree in a desert desperately fighting to survive and flourish. I told them that I was a Christian and asked if I could share what I felt God was saying.

'Of course' they said, 'please do.'

When I did, they both welled up, so I asked them gently if I could pray for them. Without saying a word we grabbed hands as I quickly scanned for security guards. I bowed my head and prayed.

Two days later they attended our dinner where my friend Phillip spoke on *Knowing God*. They responded in choosing to follow Jesus.

*

Those arches dared me to enter, and I did, but it could have been another night at a crowded table with pleasant, yet insignificant conversations. Instead, it had been a divine moment of critical intervention for two spiritually-thirsty students.

What if I had doubted Jesus' promise to make me a fisher, or if I had rushed in, business as usual, faithful to the plan but less faithful to follow Him? I would have missed the moment when my readiness to share collided with their readiness to respond. A level of readiness is unlocked when you know who you are and what you've been made for – when you know that you are a fisher, made to fish.

Let's investigate a little more deeply what Jesus meant when He said, '*Follow me and I will make you...*'

MADE TO FISH

'*And Jesus, walking by the Sea of Galilee, saw two brothers, Simon called Peter, and Andrew his brother, casting a net into the sea; for they were fishermen. Then He said to them, "Follow Me, and* ***I will make you*** *fishers of men"*' (Matthew 4:18-19 NKJV, my emphasis).

Jesus said three things to these two brothers who were fishermen. Firstly, to follow Him; secondly, He would make them into something, and thirdly, that He would make them into fishers of men.

Does what Jesus said to them apply to you? If you are a follower of Jesus, then the answer is yes.

To be clear, this is not a duty to fulfil – it is a joy to experience. To be made a fisher means you are empowered to be who you are when you engage in sharing your faith. Sharing your faith is not trying to force yourself to do something you are not made for. It is functioning in your design.

But you might respond by saying, 'Frans, I'm not an evangelist!' I have heard people say this, and what they mean is that they are called to other areas of ministry such as pastoral ministry, or perhaps administration, or any of the other valuable areas of ministry mentioned in the Bible.

Dr Rice Broocks, in his doctoral study on the gift of the evangelist, outlines the definition and function of the evangelist. Based on a careful study of scripture he defines the evangelist as follows:

> ...the ministry gift given by the Holy Spirit to men and women to preach the gospel to unbelievers and to **equip other believers to do the same**, while leading the entire community of faith (to which they are connected) to expand their borders as well as plant new churches. One of the factors that adds to the confusion about the gift of the evangelist is the **mistaken notion that there is a spiritual gift of evangelism.**[1] (My emphasis.)

He further adds,

> For the most part the perception has been that the super-hero, great man of God is going to swoop in and do the job for the struggling bedraggled church. While the evangelist will necessarily come into a particular context and use their grace and gift to give a supernatural lift to God's people, **the ultimate blessing will come when the people of God are empowered so that when the evangelist leaves, people are able to more effectively evangelize within their own community.**[2] (My emphasis.)

Dr Rice Broocks applies verses like Ephesians 4:12 and 13 to derive this definition. Ephesians 4 explains that the evangelist, together with other ministry offices, are given to the church to equip believers for the works of the ministry.

Biblically then, if you say you are not an evangelist (and you may be right), what you mean is that you are not called to equip the saints for evangelism ministry, but you are needing to be equipped and empowered by an evangelist to become effective in the ministry of evangelism.

Are you not convinced yet? That's okay, let's look a little further.

In Matthew 10 when Jesus sent out the twelve disciples on a mission, He didn't separate those called as evangelists from those called to other areas of ministry. Or for that matter, He didn't only send the ones where He had specified that He would make them into fishers of men. He sent all twelve followers to go and share the good news of the Kingdom.

The same applies when Jesus sent out the seventy-two in Luke 10; and in Matthew 28, when Jesus gives the Great Commission to the eleven remaining disciples, *all* are commissioned to go into all the world to make disciples of every nation. In Acts 1:8 when Jesus promises the Holy Spirit (who will provide the power necessary to be His witness in Jerusalem and to all the world), the promise is made to all who gathered at His ascension. He makes no distinction.

So, although He may not have specified to all followers that He will make them fishers, He does send all to fish. His promise to them is a promise to you; He is making you into a fisher of men. That is good news.

Let's dive in and look more deeply at the three things Jesus said to Peter and Andrew.

FOLLOW ME

The first instruction he gave the brothers is to *follow* Him before promising to make them into something. This is important. If you don't follow Jesus, He can't make you into a fisher of men.

Imagine if Jesus, in His carpenter days, wanted to make a chair, but the wood He required for this project wasn't available. Since the wood is not available, He would not be able to make that chair. Jesus wants to make you and shape you. He has amazing plans and purposes for your life. But the principle here is that for Him to make you and lead you into the purposes and plans He has for you, you need to be available by following Him. You need to be accessible to Him. That means to submit to Him and obey Him; it means that He becomes the Lord of your life. He is your king and your loving master. You learn from Him, and you obey His instructions and His commands. When you follow Him, and obey Him, then He can make you and shape you into what He has purposed for you.

This is why *abiding,* as outlined in chapter two, is so important as a foundation for sharing your faith. Abiding in God's Word shapes you. Abiding in His presence through worship and prayer shapes you. Abiding in community with other followers shapes you. The Word of God, the presence of God, and being part of a missional community of believers will inform, inspire and empower you into God's mission to save the world.

I WILL MAKE YOU

The word *make* in Matthew 4:19 is from the Greek word *poieō*, which means 'to make or fashion something out of existing material'.

The person who said, '*I will make you...*' was a carpenter. Think about that for a moment; He knew something about making things. Jesus could take a piece of wood and turn it into many things. It could be a table, or a chair, a bowl, a vase, a door, and the list goes on. The purpose He had in mind would determine the design, and contribution of the thing He was making. A table contributes by providing a surface for all kinds of functions. A chair contributes by providing a place for people to sit, and so on.

In Matthew 4, Jesus is not talking about wood, but people. Throughout the New Testament we see that God wants to make us and shape us for meaningful and wonderful contributions to the world. Ephesians 2:10 talks about us being God's workmanship; we are created for good works, which have been prepared in advance for us. Isaiah 64:8 refers to God as a potter and we as the clay that He is shaping for His purposes, a metaphor used a few times in the Old and New Testaments.

God wants you to participate in His mission to bring restoration to all that has been lost and broken in His beautiful creation. You can contribute in many meaningful ways: you can care for the needy, you can give generously towards the mission of your church, you can pray, lead, and be hospitable. The list is endless. In other words, you can contribute your gifts, abilities and skills to reach ready hearts to respond to the good news of Jesus.

Here in Matthew 4, Jesus is specific about what He will make you into.

FISHERS OF MEN

Jesus said, *'...I will make you into fishers of men.'* He promised Peter and Andrew a purpose, and function: to be fishers of men. But what exactly did He mean by *fishers of men*? I don't think we need to elaborate too extensively. I hope we can agree He meant they would help people who were not followers of Jesus to become followers. In other words, to reach the lost.

(In case you get stuck on the word *men*, the good news is the Greek word here is *anthrōpos*, which would be more accurately translated *humankind*. In other words, they are made to reach both women and men. Throughout the New Testament we see the followers of Jesus reaching men and women.)

If you go to the trouble of making something for a specified purpose, then you will use it for that purpose. Think about a toaster and a kettle. If they stay in the cupboard, you miss out on their contributions. At the same time, you don't use a toaster to boil water; you will destroy it. You don't use a kettle to make toast.

If you are not fishing, then there are abilities you have that are either dormant, or being misused. But there is something so glorious when you become, and do what you were made for.

A CALL TO ALL

The world is lost and broken, but there is hope. The promised Kingdom of God is here and accessible through faith in Jesus. The world needs to know, but the nets in the boat will not catch the fish. When you say, ‘Yes, I am made to fish! Yes, I will fish! Jesus, how do you want me to fish?’, He joins you to others, also fishing, and together we become the net.

Everyone knows someone who is not yet a follower of Jesus. The someone you know is someone I may never be able to reach. You are part of the net that can reach the fish that others are not positioned to reach. If every follower becomes a fisher, the net gets bigger and stronger, and more people will be reached.

How will they know unless you go? Say, ‘Here I am Lord, send me!’

CONCLUSION: CULTIVATING YOUR WILLINGNESS THROUGH BEING

When you know your identity and your design, and have clarity about your calling, you can function and contribute accordingly. What you do flows from who you are. This is what I mean by *being*. Being who you are, and doing accordingly. Think back to when I faced those arches in Paris, taunting me and daunting me. I reminded myself that I had been made to fish and I am a fisher of men! I called on Jesus to help me fish according to the promise He made to make me a fisher. That was a prayer of faith that catalysed me into a significant fishing moment as I put my trust in Him and what He had made me to be. Jesus has done the same for you. As you follow Him, He is making you a fisher too.

Can you commit to follow Jesus and let Him 'make you'? Can you embrace your identity and design to be a fisher of men? By embracing your identity of being a fisher you are raising your readiness through impacting your willingness.

Next, you will discover the enormous difference it makes when you do what you do for the right reason, and let love lead.

CHAPTER FOUR

WILLINGNESS FROM COMPASSION

At first, I did not appreciate the interruption. Deb and I had planned the morning for productive focus with military-like precision. With kids checked in at the crèche, and coffees ordered, we were vigorously typing away on our laptops when he approached the table. I looked up to see a wizened face crowned with wispy grey hair and intense blue eyes. His words were laboured and slow but fully coherent as he asked with a gentle smile, ‘sorry to disturb you, but can I ask you a question about your computer?’

My head said no! (I’m busy), but my heart said yes, as I could see the appeal in his eyes for help. My heart won, and I invited him to sit down as he introduced himself as Dave. ‘I’ve just got a Mac’ he told me, ‘but I’m struggling to find how to do what I know how to do on my PC.’

It turned out Dave had bought his computer from a store my brother owned, so I asked him whether he knew that they offered free conversion courses with the purchase. He did know, but said it wouldn’t help him. ‘You see I’ve had five brain tumours removed, which has affected my ability to learn.’

I could see the desperation in his eyes as he patiently waited for my response. My heart was moved with compassion as I considered the journey, the struggle, the pain, the uncertainty that he must have gone through, the challenge of facing one battle after another between an invasive disease and multiple life-threatening surgeries that left him impaired in his learning ability.

'Dave, I hope you don't mind me asking, but has anyone prayed for you?'

'Yes, they have, but nothing happened.'

At first, I wasn't sure what to say next. I prayed before proceeding. 'I imagine that would raise some questions, and could be confusing.' He nodded ever so slightly.

'Has anyone tried answering your questions about God, or healing?' He shook his head.

'Would you mind if I tried? I can't guarantee that I will have the answers you need but I am willing to try.'

'I would really like that.' Dave said.

Not only had he struggled with brain tumours but six months prior to our conversation, his wife had passed away. The pain of his wife's death and the struggle with multiple surgeries had triggered his enquiries about God. After I outlined the gospel, with tears streaming down his wrinkly cheeks, he prayed, repented and received Jesus as His Lord and saviour. More than sixty years of rejecting God wiped away as His loving heavenly Father received him into His family.

About a year later, Dave called me up the night before he went in for a sixth surgery. I will never forget what he shared. 'Frans, for the first time I'm going to the operating table with peace in my heart because I know Jesus is with me, and I know where I'm going if I don't make it.'

Thankfully Dave survived the surgery and continued loving and serving the SAVIOUR he had rejected for so long.

*

With Deb and I intent on a productive morning, it was tempting to treat Dave's questions like a disruptive intrusion; I could have turned him away. His age, and need to master new technology, prompted me with enough empathy to help, although I recall feeling a bit hassled initially. But the real trigger came when Dave shared about his health challenges and his wife passing away; my heart was deeply moved with compassion and that motivated me to engage him further. The love and compassion in my heart conquered the busyness that threatened to rob me of the powerful eternal moment I had the privilege to share with him.

Busyness will defeat our willingness, but love and compassion will defeat busyness. Busyness is not the only barrier to sharing our faith – indifference, intimidation and distraction, to name just a few, can handbrake us from putting on our shoes of readiness and stepping out. But love and compassion can defeat any, and every one of these.

If this is true, it will help to better understand love and compassion so that we can harness their potential to empower us to lean into these incredible eternal opportunities.

ACTION FROM COMPASSION

Why is it that compassion can trigger your willingness for sharing your faith? According to the University of California, 'Greater Good Science Centre', compassion can be described as: 'To suffer together. Among emotion-researchers, it is defined as the feeling that arises when you are confronted with another's suffering and feel motivated to relieve that suffering.'[1] I like that word motivated, and how compassion is 'being motivated to relieve suffering'. You see, sin in a soul produces suffering.

Your neighbour, or friend who does not know Jesus is made to be God's image bearer and to reflect His holiness. They are made to walk in love, joy, peace, and in His goodness, and ultimately in a life-giving relationship with their creator. But the sin in their life separates them from God and His goodness.

Think back to Dave. While he suffered trauma due to the loss of his wife and in his fight with a frightening, life-threatening disease, he did not have the benefit we have of experiencing and knowing the '*peace of God that surpasses all understanding guarding our hearts and minds'* (Philippians 4:7). He also did not have the security of knowing, with assurance, what would happen to him if he didn't survive one of the many life-threatening surgeries he had to face.

Corruption through sin produces death in us – a spiritual death that results in pain, corruption, guilt, shame, confusion, arrogance, relational separation, insecurity, insignificance and so much more.

My good friend, Jonathan Rens, has written articles on what he calls *soul-ache*. Soul-ache is that gnawing emptiness and pain in the soul that is the consequence of a life lived without God devastated by the brokenness in this world and the consequences of our sinful choices. When you truly grasp the human condition and the desperate state we are in without God, both in this life and the next, there is an opportunity to be moved with compassion into action to share your faith.

My hope is that, as an image bearer of a loving creator, your heart gets stirred to care about your neighbour, family, friend or even a stranger, and that your willingness to share your faith is triggered.

We have focused on compassion, but there is something even greater than compassion that is the driving force behind it: love. Let us first examine why it's important, and secondly, how to cultivate it in our hearts.

THE IMPORTANCE OF LOVE

We all have barriers to sharing our faith. Some of us have had awful experiences when giving it a go. Love is a powerful and significant ingredient that can demolish these barriers and produce beautiful experiences of engaging people with the good news of Jesus.

1 Corinthians 16:14 says *'Do everything in love.'* Everything means everything. Everything includes sharing your faith.

The apostle Paul profoundly describes love to a group of believers living in the ancient Greek city of Corinth:

> *Love is patient and kind; love does not envy or boast; it is not arrogant or rude. It does not insist on its own way; it is not irritable or resentful; it does not rejoice at wrongdoing but rejoices with the truth. Love bears all things, hopes all things, endures all things.*
>
> 1 Corinthians 13:4-6 ESV

Patience and kindness are amazing qualities with which to engage conversations about faith. Boasting, arrogance and rudeness are not. Paul's definition of love also addresses not being judgemental or harsh about the truth, and people's wrongdoings or wrong beliefs. Not giving up on people, even when they are resistant and not responding immediately, is addressed as he exhorts us to bear, hope and endure all things. What a profound and beautiful encouragement to bring love to the centre of our approach when we engage people with the good news of Jesus!

I want to present to you three reasons why you need love for effective evangelism. Firstly, love cultivates willingness. Secondly, love defeats barriers to your willingness. Thirdly, love, or its lack, will leave an impression

Deb and I have seen many people who were dormant activated because they grasped the significance of love as a motivator for sharing their faith. I am trusting you can experience the same. Let's look at each of these three reasons.

1. LOVE CULTIVATES WILLINGNESS

When Deb and I were engaged, I was living in London, and she lived about 260 kilometres (162 miles) away in Exeter. It was her birthday, so I spoke to my boss and he allowed me to finish work early. As a surprise, I bought a train ticket and arranged with her dad to pick me up from the station.

In the car, on our way to their home, I phoned Deb to wish her happy birthday, and while we were talking, I quietly entered the house and opened the door where she was on the phone talking to me. She looked straight at me and carried on talking, not realising I was standing right there! Her expression was priceless when the realisation dawned that I wasn't 260 kilometres away, but standing just two metres in front of her.

Why did I go to all the effort and expense for such an elaborate surprise? Quite simply, because I loved her. I'm not saying that you need romantic love to share the good news of Jesus with someone! But the principle is that love will motivate you to do what you otherwise wouldn't want to.

I heard someone share once that indifference finds an excuse, but love makes a way. It is like when you don't want to do something that you need to do. Suddenly the household chores you normally put off become very appealing; they become great distractions from doing what you need to do. Likewise, we can find all sorts of reasons for *not* sharing our faith. Love, however, is a powerful force for overcoming our comforts and conveniences. You see, busyness, indifference, intimidation, fear and most likely every barrier you identify to sharing your faith, is rooted in self. When your focus is on yourself and your own needs, and not on the needs of others, you will always default to what is best for you. But when you love another, you will sacrifice for what is best for them. In my case, whether it was choosing not to stay conveniently in London on my fiancé's birthday, or responding to an elderly gentleman's questions in a coffee shop, love triggered the ability to sacrifice my conveniences and comforts for their benefit. Love conquers barriers that stand in the way of you sharing your faith.

Aren't you thankful that God, at an enormous cost to Himself, left the comforts of heaven and suffered an excruciating, sinless death on a splintered Roman cross, all because of how much He loves you? Love made a way where indifference could have found an excuse.

2. LOVE DEFEATS BARRIERS

One of the remarkable things about God is that He cares about the state of our hearts – the emotional, spiritual, volitional (our will) dimension of our being – more than just our actions. He is not just concerned with us doing the right thing, but doing it for the right reason.

Before the apostle Paul outlines the qualities of love in the chapter I referred to earlier, he makes this point:

> *If I speak in the tongue of men and of angels, but have not love, I am a noisy gong or a clanging cymbal. And if I have prophetic powers, and understand all mysteries and all knowledge, and if I have all faith, so as to remove mountains, but have not love, I am nothing. If I give away all I have, and if I give up my body to be burned, but have not love, I gain nothing.*
>
> 1 Corinthians 13:1-3 ESV

Wow! That seems harsh. Huge generosity, martyrdom, gigantic faith, operating powerfully with spiritual gifts, is all meaningless without love. It's not harsh at all. God honours all these actions, but only when they are offered with sacrificial love, and not selfish pride. And the cherry on top is that when we do these things in love, there is a joy that comes that is absent when we do them only for ourselves.

When sharing our faith, we can do so out of duty, obligation and compulsion, or we can do so with love, care and compassion. Doing the right thing for the right reason can be a struggle. Over the years I have ministered to Christians who've battled with feelings of not being good enough, or they have struggled with wanting to be liked and accepted. Some have battled with always feeling like an outsider, like they could never really belong, whether in their own family, their workplace, social circle or church. These feelings of insecurity and uncertainty can quickly translate to seeking approval and belonging through performance and achievement.

Sharing our faith can become an arena where unwholesome and unhelpful motives can distort why we do what we do. You can be deceived into thinking that if you work hard and achieve enough, then you will be loved and accepted. This thinking can apply to seeking approval and love from both God and people.

The good news is, that by God's glorious grace, we can and should be liberated from the burden of seeking approval through performance. Whether you share the gospel, and lead people to Christ or not, this does not determine how much God loves you.

When we share our faith with the right motive, there are benefits for both us and the people we have conversations with.

3. LOVE, OR ITS LACK, WILL LEAVE AN IMPRESSION

God doesn't want us sharing our faith without wanting to. When our hearts are gripped with God's heart and His love for people, it changes the attitude with which we share.

John Maxwell, popular author and speaker, stated that 'People may hear your words, but they feel your attitude.'[2] What do you want them to feel when you tell them the good news that God loves them? Do they experience the love you are talking about? God doesn't just want them to know about His love, He wants them to experience His love. He can do that through you.

I was doing a training with my good friend and amazing evangelist, Rudzani Mulaudzi, and he made a powerful statement about sharing our faith, which stuck with me. He said: 'People will forget what you said, but will remember how they felt.'

When our hearts and motives are filled with love, then our attitude of love is what they will experience and remember. But when love is absent, they will experience that too.

In 2008, there was a xenophobic crisis in South Africa that displaced over 40,000 people overnight. I was part of a team that helped more than 1500 people in our surrounding communities. For three weeks, over 800 people lived in our church building, sleeping on mattresses on the floor. I oversaw a team of volunteers who registered every person as they arrived on our doorstep. The people seeking shelter were traumatised; their lives had been threatened, and many had escaped their homes with just the clothes on their backs.

I was so repulsed when I saw one of our leaders treating these precious, fear-filled souls with contempt. This person was rude and abrasive and completely insensitive to what they had been through. Clearly, they felt inconvenienced to give up a couple of hours to help with registration. All they could think about was themselves, and as a result they robbed themselves of an opportunity to serve, love and bless these precious people, many of whom were not yet followers of Jesus. I immediately relieved them of their 'duty' and sent them home. They missed out on an opportunity to love and to serve like Jesus instructed us to. Thankfully, despite that person's attitude, God used the situation, and over the three weeks many of those we cared for made commitments to follow Jesus.

We overcome the barriers to our willingness when we do all these things in love. You will do what you do with the purest and most wonderful of motives, and your experience and the experience of those to whom you speak, will be a powerfully positive one.

This leads us to the next vital question: how do you access the powerful forces of love and compassion that defy the enemies of your willingness?

HOW TO WALK IN THE WAY OF LOVE

Here are two simple, but vital means for growing the love you need for cultivating your willingness.

1. RECEIVE

My teenage years were fraught with pain, confusion and struggle. My parents divorced when I was eight-years old, and from thirteen to twenty, I never saw or heard from my dad. At times people who tried to love me bore the brunt of my confusion, anger, and bitterness. One friend in particular, Danny, for reasons that are beyond me, decided he would love me no matter how badly I treated him.

One day, when I was about sixteen-years old, I swore and shouted at Danny for something he had done that had not warranted such a malicious attack. He stood on our doorstep with tears streaming down his cheeks. With nothing but love in his eyes, he wiped his tears, and said that he still cared about me and would not stop being my friend no matter what I did or said. He was true to his word. That day, a layer of hardness broke in my heart as he demonstrated God's unconditional love for me. With great patience, endurance and kindness, Danny modelled true friendship and love that eventually brought healing and liberation to my wounded and broken soul. I learnt to receive God's love through him in a way that released that same love to flow through me.

1 John 4:19 says, *'We love because he first loved us.'* It is difficult to love others if we have not first received love for ourselves. We can't give what we have not received. You may not have a Danny in your life like I did, but you do have Jesus. One thing I know is that Jesus has demonstrated how much He loves you by giving up His life for you. Like He said, there is no greater love than to lay down one's life for a friend, and while we were still sinners, in rebellion to God, Christ died for us (Romans 5:8). There is nothing more God can do to show you just how much He loves you. If you struggle to receive and experience His love, then you can still receive it by faith, trusting in what He has said in His Word and done for you. You can pray and ask Him to show you His love. Push aside the thoughts and arguments that contradict the truth of His love. The enemy has many lies and deceptions designed to convince us we are not loved. But God's Word is powerful to demolish those lies if

we will choose to believe what God says, and distrust what we think or feel.

So, to cultivate love and compassion, start by receiving God's love that is already freely available.

2. PERCEIVE

Have you ever met someone you found annoying initially, but when you got to know them, you ended up becoming good friends? Funnily enough, Danny, my friend whom I mentioned previously, was such a guy. I still remember the first time I met him when a mutual friend invited us to watch a movie. I found his jokes annoying, his laugh irritating, and I was glad when the evening was over. My brother thought he was cool and said I should get to know him. The common ground between us was surfing. Through surfing we started to hang out, and I discovered my brother was right.

The principle here is to *perceive*. Open your eyes and observe what is going on in people's lives. Spend time with them. Pray for them. Allow yourself to see them as God sees them and as you do you may find God's love for them bubbling up in your heart.

In Colossians 4:3, the apostle Paul asks the believers to pray for him for open doors for the gospel, and then he says, *'be watchful'*. That's an instruction to perceive. Look and observe what God is doing in response to your prayers. Even praying is part of perceiving because God can download to you how He sees the people you are praying for. You can perceive the brokenness and struggle in people's lives because of their sin. This can trigger the compassion that triggers your willingness. You can perceive God's glorious plans and purposes for their lives. You can perceive what the Father is doing and come alongside the good work He has already begun in them. You can perceive the sin that is destroying them.

We will unpack the principle, and process for perceiving in greater depth in Chapter ten.

So, starting with receiving love ourselves, we intentionally lift our eyes and look at the harvest to perceive and see others as God sees them.

CONCLUSION: CULTIVATING YOUR WILLINGNESS THROUGH COMPASSION

Danny, in my broken teenage years, was like the hands, feet and voice of Jesus in my life in the way he loved me unconditionally, broke through my barriers of anger and bitterness to get through to me that I was truly loved. This paved the way for healing and wholeness in my soul as he pointed me to God's love and the healing available to me through the ministry of Jesus. You can be the hands, feet and voice of Jesus in the lives of others. If you are willing to receive God's love in your heart, and with a heart filled with love, you can perceive the brokenness in others that you once had, then compassion can conquer any barriers to your willingness.

God doesn't want you sharing your faith out of obligation. Sharing your faith out of obligation is unpleasant for you, and the person you're sharing with. It's a loss for everyone. However, when compulsion is replaced with compassion, everyone wins.

God also doesn't want you sharing your faith to try prove something either. To try gain approval or acceptance through accomplishments is exhausting, and it's not sustainable. You will inevitably grow weary in doing good. When you know that you are loved by God, and that He cannot possibly love you more than He already does, this liberates you to love others as He loves you. Then, everything you do for God is from a heart of worship and gratitude. Think of Jesus when He was water baptised by His cousin, John. The Father declared, *'this is my beloved Son with whom I am well pleased.'* Jesus was approved by His Father before He started His earthly ministry! That is significant.

When our hearts are filled with the knowledge that God loves us, eternal moments, like with Dave in the coffee shop, become available and accessible.

*

In this section we have looked at how to cultivate our willingness to share our faith. God can do more with an untrained person who is willing, than with a professional who is not willing. If you still feel unwilling, go back to the ABCs of Abiding, Being and Compassion. We grow willingness through prioritising time spent with Jesus (abiding), by recognising that we are made to fish – that it is not something separate from our divine design (being) – and by perceiving people with compassion as we receive and affirm ourselves in God's unconditional love.

What if someone you know becomes curious about your faith? Would you know what to share with them? We have the most profound, life-impacting, glorious good news to proclaim.

In Section Two, we will explore what the good news is and how to share it. My hope is that you will grasp the *magnificence* of God, the full *meaning* of sin and its consequences, and the incredible *magnitude* of God's restoration plan.

SECTION TWO

COMMUNICATION

YOUR NOTES

CHAPTER FIVE

THE TREASURE WE GET TO SHARE

Deb and I live in one of the most exciting cities in the world. London is a hub for business, education, and life itself! Nearly ten million people live here, representing more than 180 nations, with over 300 languages spoken. Sometimes it feels like the whole world passes through this city. At other times, God sends us out to the world – recently I had the opportunity to take the gospel to children in Ukraine scarred by war, to China with students weighing up the risks of faith and to families in Belfast trying to break free from prejudice and violence.

Wherever we are, one thing remains constant, the good news of Jesus Christ. Our motivation is simple – *For God so loved the world...* (John 3:16). And whether people are coming to us or we are going to them, one question matters most: how will we communicate the gospel?

That's what this section of the book is about. If the first part – *Preparation* – was about cultivating readiness in our hearts, this part – *Communication* – is about the message itself. What exactly do we say when the moment comes? And how can we share it in a way that is clear, compelling, and full of life?

The good news is this: you are more ready than you think.

*

Let me take you to the ocean for a moment.

I was paddling into dangerous surf with two good friends, Steve and Dougal. The waves were monstrous that day – walls of water pounding the Cape Town coastline, waves that could drag you under until your lungs ached for air. But Steve had another struggle. He was pale, still reeling from a heavy night of drinking following a fight with his wife. Something in me sensed God was preparing more than just a surf session. I began praying for him.

Weeks later, suiting up at another big wave surf spot, Steve turned to me with the question that had been stirring in him, 'Tell me about your faith.'

My heart pounded as I told him about Jesus – the one who offers forgiveness, freedom, and a fresh start. Right there, Steve said yes to Him. His life changed dramatically. Addiction lost its grip. Anger gave way to peace. His marriage found new ground.

Not long after that, at a barbecue, Steve shared his story with a group of surfers. His voice trembled as he spoke of the freedom and joy Jesus had brought. The room fell silent. One of the guys, Daniel, was so moved he later prayed with Dougal out in the surf and gave his life to Christ too.

Two friends. Two lives. Two eternities transformed.

Here's the point: Steve and Daniel aren't unusual. You and I also move in circles – workplaces, gyms, classrooms, cafés, neighbourhoods – where people are closer to faith than we might think. Like them, many are ready for good news. All they need is someone ready to share.

THE TREASURE IN THE FIELD

Jesus once described the gospel this way: *'The kingdom of heaven is like* ***treasure hidden in a field****. When a man found it, he hid it again, and then* ***in his joy*** *went and sold all he had and bought that field.'* (Matthew 13:44, my emphasis)

Notice the man's reaction: joy.

The gospel is not bad news disguised as good. It is the most valuable treasure anyone can ever discover. It brings forgiveness for guilt, freedom from shame, healing for brokenness, and hope for eternity. No wonder Paul could write: *'For I am not ashamed of the gospel, because it is the power of God that brings salvation to everyone who believes.'* (Romans 1:16)

If you were selling an expensive diamond ring, you wouldn't just point out the gold band – you'd hold it up to the light so everyone could see the brilliance of the diamond. That's what shows its true worth. The gospel is like that. It's not just a story, not just another opinion in a noisy world. It is a treasure of immeasurable value.

Clarity matters. Courage matters. Communication matters.

This message is not just information – it is power. It transforms lives. And it is worth giving everything for.

THE GOSPEL STEPS

So how do we communicate this treasure in a way that is simple, memorable, and true to the heart of the message?

That's why we use *Gospel Steps* – to help us hold up the diamond ring of the gospel so people can see its beauty and grasp it's profound truth. In these simple steps we share who God is and what He has done for us. We want people to grasp not just what they are saved *from* – the devastating impact of sin – but also what they are saved *for* – a life of purpose, hope, and meaning that begins now and lasts into eternity. The steps are simple:

1. Step 1: God.
2. Step 2: Sin.
3. Step 3: Restoration.

Each step is represented by two symbols to make the truth easy to see, easy to share, and easy to remember.

STEP 1: GOD

GOD IS LOVE

God is love. His very nature is love, and He created us in His image to be in relationship with Him. He is compassionate and kind, caring deeply about the brokenness in the world and about each one of us. (1 John 4:16; Genesis 1:26-27; John 3:16).

GOD IS KING

God is also King – the King of kings. His reign is marked by holiness, justice, and truth. He rules not as a tyrant, but as a good and righteous King who will one day set everything right. (Psalm 47:2-3; Revelation 4:11).

STEP 2: SIN

THE CAUSE AND CONSEQUENCE OF SIN

Sin is rejecting God's holiness and design, like a wrong answer on a test. It separates us from Him and brings brokenness and death into our lives and the world. (Romans 3:23; Isaiah 59:2).

JESUS DEFEATED SIN

God's answer to sin was Jesus. He lived the life we could not live, died the death we deserved, and rose again victorious over sin, death, and the devil. The cross is the greatest demonstration of God's love and justice, opening the way back to Him. (Colossians 2:13-15; John 3:16).

STEP 3: RESTORATION

I MUST TURN FROM SIN AND TURN TO GOD

Restoration begins with repentance – turning away from sin and turning back to God. Through Jesus, we are forgiven, born again, and welcomed into God's family. (Acts 3:19; Luke 15:17-24).

I AM RESTORED TO RULE

God doesn't just forgive us; He restores us to our original calling – to reign with Him as His image -bearers, living as His ambassadors in this world. We carry His authority, steward His creation, and live with purpose until the day He returns to restore all things. (Romans 5:17; Genesis 1:26-28).

CONCLUSION: CLEAR AND COMPELLING COMMUNICATION

The apostle Paul said it like this:

> *Now, brothers and sisters, I want to remind you of* ***the gospel I preached to you****, which you received and on which you have taken your stand.* ***By this gospel you are saved****, if you hold firmly to the word I preached to you. Otherwise, you have believed in vain. For what I received I passed on to you* ***as of first importance:*** *that* ***Christ died for our sins*** *according to the Scriptures, that he* ***was buried****, that he* ***was raised on the third day*** *according to the Scriptures.*
>
> 1 Corinthians 15:1-4 (my emphasis)

Paul was writing to believers in Corinth – a bustling city full of diversity, culture, and competing ideas. Sound familiar? Much like London today or our online digital world. He reminded them of what mattered most: the gospel. He called it *'of first importance'* because it is the foundation of everything. And then he made it crystal clear: *Christ died for our sins, He was buried, and He rose again* – just as the Scriptures foretold.

That is the gospel. That is the power of God for salvation. That is the treasure we get to carry into our conversations.

And here's the good news: you don't have to be a preacher or a theologian to share it. Just like surfers Steve and Daniel discovered Christ through the everyday faith of friends, the people around you -your neighbours, colleagues, classmates, teammates, even family members – are often more ready than you think. God has placed you in circles of influence where His light can shine through you.

That's why Paul urges us to put on *'the shoes of readiness that come from the gospel of peace'*. It's about being prepared to step into ordinary moments with extraordinary hope.

So where do we begin? If the gospel is a story, the first chapter is God Himself. Before we can talk about sin, or even restoration, we need a clear and compelling vision of who God is. Because when people see Him as He really is – loving, holy, and just – they begin to realise why knowing Him is worth everything.

That's where we'll start: the magnificence of God.

YOUR NOTES

CHAPTER SIX

STEP 1: THE MAGNIFICENCE OF GOD

'How can you say he was born of a virgin?' Looking into his youthful eyes I could see Jack's question was sincere and not hostile. I glanced at Deb working at the kitchen table. The kids were already in bed, Jack and I were enjoying the warm summer evening relaxing on the sofa. I could tell she'd heard the direction of the conversation. The nod she gave indicated my back was covered, no doubt she was already praying quietly.

For the next forty minutes I fielded his questions, which went far and wide. He was deep in thought and clearly had been puzzling these questions for some time. I sensed that like myself, he was thankful for the opportunity for this conversation.

'Would you like to experience the God we are talking about, Jack?'

With his permission I prayed for him, my hand gently on his shoulder: 'God, I know you love Jack; please would you show him that you are real and that you love him.'

Suddenly his body began to shake, and tears were streaming down his cheeks. I waited. Then, with a big sigh he opened his eyes.

'What just happened, Jack?'

'It was crazy, I felt this power going through me, like electricity, and I had an overwhelming peace like I've never experienced before. It was so amazing.'

'Do you know what that is?'

'No, but I want to.'

'Do you mind if I explain to you who God is and what he's done for us?

After ministering the gospel, he accepted the invitation to repent and put his trust in Jesus. As we prayed, the same thing happened again, he began to shake and weep as he accepted Jesus as Lord and Saviour.

*

Not everyone encounters God in such a dramatic way. But for whatever reason, that night Jack did. God showed up in a way that touched him deeply. It was powerful. And yet, as amazing as that moment was, it wasn't enough on its own. Jack still needed to understand who God is – in a way that made sense, a way that would give him the confidence to put his trust in Christ.

That's true for so many people today. In our world, some are completely unaware of who God really is. Others carry distorted pictures of Him -harsh, distant, irrelevant, or imaginary.

Centuries ago, the French philosopher Blaise Pascal saw the same problem in his own culture. He wrote:

'Men despise religion. They hate it and are afraid it may be true. The cure for this is first to show that religion is not contrary to reason, but worthy of reverence and respect. Next, make it attractive, make good men wish it were true, and then show that it is.' Put simply: we persuade that *God is real* and that He is *reasonable, desirable* and *worthy*.

That's the task in front of us. We are not just defending ideas. We are pointing to a treasure – a treasure worth giving everything to obtain, as Jesus said in one of His parables in Matthew 13:44.

What a treasure He is. God is beyond comprehension; magnificent, majestic, glorious, wonderful. And yet He bends low to love His creation. That's where we begin – with His goodness and His nature. As Pascal reminded us, we start by showing why God is worth knowing, why knowing Him is worth everything.

GOD IS LOVE

And so we know and rely on the love
God has for us. ***God is love****.*
Whoever lives in love lives in God, and God in them.
1 John 4:16 (my emphasis)

One of the most life-changing truths I've ever discovered is this: *God is love.* Not just that He sometimes shows love, or that He chooses to love certain people – but that love is His very nature. He cannot help but love, because it's who He is.

I remember holding each of my children for the very first time when they were born. They hadn't done anything to earn my love. They couldn't even speak or smile yet. They demanded sleepless nights, smelly tasks and added expensive line items to our budget. But the love I felt for them was so deep, so fierce, that I would have done anything for them in that moment. That's the closest picture I can give of how God feels toward us – but His love is even greater.

And the beautiful thing is, His love isn't generic. It's not like a blanket He throws over the whole world without noticing the details. Just as each of my children is completely unique, God loves us individually. My son Titus loves to analyse and think everything through, while Ethan is more of a dive-in-and-figure-it-out kind of guy. My daughter Ruth has her own personality again, nothing like her brothers. As their father, I love each of them not despite their differences but because of them. That's how God sees you – unique, special, loved for who you are.

The Bible says, *'God is love. Whoever lives in love lives in God, and God in them'*. That means you are not forgotten, not a mistake, not unloved. The God who created the galaxies knows your name and loves you more than you could ever imagine.

I've seen this love in action in ways that have shaken me to the core. In March 2025, my daughter and I participated as volunteers at a youth camp in Ukraine organised by our good friends, Kostya and Aya. Many of the children had lost parents in the war. Some had family members fighting on the frontlines. When I looked into their eyes, I wondered what I could possibly say to comfort them. And yet, as I shared with them about God's love – that He loved them regardless of their choices, regardless of their pain, and that nothing could make Him stop loving them – I could see something change. They were hearing, maybe for the first time, that there is a God who loves them with a love that can never be broken.

This is why Jesus came as stated in His own words: *'For God so loved the world that He gave His one and only Son.'*

(John 3:16). His love is the reason He gave everything. And His love is the reason He still reaches out to you and me today.

GOD IS KING

*Clap your hands, all you nations; Shout to God with cries of joy. For the Lord most high is awesome, **the great King** over all the earth.*
Psalm 47:2-3 (my emphasis)

But God is not only love. He is also King.

For some people, that's not comforting at first. The idea of someone being in charge feels scary. I spoke to a student on campus in London, and when I was explaining the meaning of the crown in *the Gospel Steps*, she said the idea of God being King made her feel trapped, as though her freedom would be taken away. Maybe you've felt something similar?

But here's what I've learned: when the right person is in charge, it's not oppressive – it's freeing.

At school, can you remember what happened when the teacher left the classroom for an extended period? Chaos! In my school, it would lead to bloodshed! If there is no God, then might is right and the strongest determine the rules. But it also matters who is in charge, if someone is.

I had all kinds of teachers at school. Some had no control, and the classroom would descend into chaos. Others were cruel and harsh. But then there was one teacher – Mr. Street. He was strict, yes, but he was also kind and always fair. You never doubted that even when he was tough on you, it was because he wanted you to thrive. And under his leadership, I flourished. I got my best academic results with him because his authority made me better.

That's what God's rule is like – only infinitely more so. He isn't a tyrant, and He isn't absent. He is a holy King, ruling with justice, truth, and goodness. The Bible says His throne will last forever, and that His sceptre is a sceptre of justice.

The prophet Isaiah had a vision of God on His throne. He saw angels crying out, '*Holy, holy, holy is the Lord Almighty; the whole earth is full of His glory.*' (Isaiah 6:3). Isaiah was overwhelmed by the majesty and purity of it all, and he suddenly realised how small and flawed he was in comparison. That's the effect God's holiness has on us when we fully comprehend it – it opens our eyes to how different He is from us, completely perfect. God's holiness is the radiant beauty that defines every other attribute. To say that God is holy is to say He is set apart, infinitely above and beyond, in a category all His own. His holiness is dazzling light with no shadow, perfect love with no trace of selfishness, pure goodness with no hint of corruption. When we catch even the smallest glimpse of it, like Isaiah did, it shakes us to the core. Holiness is what makes God glorious, and yet it is also what makes His love for us so breathtaking – that the One who is so pure, so exalted, so utterly perfect, would choose to reach down to us.

This is good news. Because the One in charge of the universe is not corrupt, not moody, not self-serving. He is love. He is justice. He is holy. Imagine a kingdom where the King is both perfectly loving and perfectly good – that's His kingdom. And He invites us to live under that reign. That's why, presenting, God is love (the heart symbol) together with, God is King (the crown symbol) helps establish that God is both desirable and true.

CONCLUSION: GOD IS MAGNIFICENT

When Jesus taught His disciples to pray, He started like this: *'Our Father in heaven, holy is Your name. Your kingdom come, Your will be done, on earth as it is in heaven'* (Matthew 6:9-10). See the balance? God is our Father – close, approachable, loving, as represented by the heart symbol. But He is also the Holy King – reigning with justice and truth, as represented by the crown symbol.

Jesus taught us to ask for His kingdom, His reign to break into our world. That means God isn't distant. He isn't indifferent. He longs to bring the goodness and peace of heaven into our lives, our families, our communities. This is the God we get to know. The God who loves with an unfailing love. The God who rules with holiness and justice. He is magnificent beyond comprehension, and yet He bends down to love and lead us. And that changes everything.

Jack had many questions about God, and questions about the Bible that did not make sense to him. But he needed more than just intellectual answers to those questions, and more than an experience of God, as meaningful as those are. He needed to know and understand who God is, that He is loving, holy and just.

There is more for us to communicate when unveiling the magnificence of the gospel message. It relates to the human condition and our universal need to thrive. Next, we will look at Step 2 which focuses on the devastation of sin. We will outline the cause of sin, the consequence of sin and, thankfully, the solution to sin.

CHAPTER SEVEN

STEP 2: THE MEANING OF SIN

The crowd was roaring, the lights blinding, and the announcer's voice echoed through the arena: 'TROOPA, you're up in thirty minutes!'. Nathan sat with his head in his hands, panic rising in his chest. In half an hour, he was supposed to be in the ring, fighting for a Welsh kickboxing title. But instead of confidence, fear consumed him.

Rushing outside, he grabbed what he thought would give him strength – drugs stashed in his car. A hit of crack, a line of cocaine. Then, stumbling back inside in a haze, he had to be helped into the ring. Before the third round was over, he collapsed – unconscious, not from a punch, but from the poison of a life spinning out of control.

That collapse was no accident. It was the visible breaking point of years of chaos and sin. Nathan had grown up in Ely, Cardiff, in a home marked by violence, alcoholism and fear. Dyslexia left him frustrated and by his teens he was selling drugs at school, kicked out at fourteen, and spiralling fast. Music and DJ-ing took him across Europe, earning awards and fame, but cocaine had become his closest companion.

By 2020, Nathan's body was failing. His gall bladder had burst, his weight had plummeted, and he was living in a crack house, too weak to walk to the shop, too broken to see his children. Nineteen of his friends died that year from overdoses or suicides. He wanted out – but couldn't escape. That's the nature of sin. It whispers promises of freedom but delivers only slavery.

And yet, God was not finished.

Through Christians who prayed for him, shared Scripture with him, and refused to give up, hope broke through. A friend named Tim finally asked the question that changed everything: 'What's stopping you from giving your life to Jesus?' That day, Nathan prayed, and for the first time in his life, he tasted real freedom.

Everything began to change. The chains of addiction loosened. The emptiness gave way to identity. The man once called 'Troopa' by the world was now called 'child of God' by the Father. Today, Nathan is a full-time evangelist, travelling to places like Romania, hosting evangelistic nights, and sharing his story with anyone who will listen. Broken lives are being healed, people are coming to faith, and hope is spreading where despair once reigned.

And the story doesn't end there. Not long after his own conversion, Nathan phoned one of his old drug dealers to tell him he'd become a Christian. That man – hardened by the same streets, sentenced to 15 years in prison – later asked Nathan to visit him. Inside the prison walls, Nathan shared the gospel where his friend surrendered his life to Jesus. Recently, he was given a day on parole for one reason: to be water baptised. A drug dealer once enslaved by sin, now washed clean, forgiven, and following Christ.

*

The gospel is a transformative force. It offers hope to individuals facing despair, brings healing to those who are experiencing brokenness, and facilitates profound personal change. It also guides people toward new roles and positive contributions within their communities.

Here's the point: sin destroys. It looks like freedom – *Do what you want, live how you like* – but it only ever enslaves. Nathan's story shows us that what looks strong on the outside can be death on the inside. Yet the gospel is God's rescue plan. Jesus doesn't just offer advice; He offers transformation. He takes what sin has ruined and makes it new.

The world is full of Nathans – people trapped in cycles of sin, longing for hope, desperate for freedom. And the good news is this: the gospel is powerful enough to save them. As Jesus said, *'So if the Son sets you free, you will be free indeed'* (John 8:36).

You don't need to experience extreme depravity like Nathan to know the world isn't the way it should be. We see beauty, but we also see brokenness. We long for love, but we carry wounds of betrayal. Without Jesus, people chase after peace, but chaos always seems to find its way back in. Many ask, 'Why is life so hard? Why is the world so messed up?' They're not alone. The answer is bigger than most of us realise.

Knowing the cause of an illness brings clarity and allows for solutions. Similarly, understanding humanity's brokenness through sin highlights the need for Jesus as the remedy. Without a clear explanation of this condition, it's hard to convey the importance of what God has done for us through Jesus.

THE CAUSE AND CONSEQUENCE OF SIN

For all have sinned and fall short of the glory of God.
Romans 6:23

Sin begins not with us, but with an enemy. The Bible tells us of a fallen being – once radiant but now consumed by pride – who set himself against God. He's called the devil, the adversary, the deceiver. His goal? To corrupt, enslave, and destroy everything good that God has made.

That's exactly what he did in the garden of Eden. He came with lies, planting seeds of doubt in Adam and Eve's hearts: *'Did God really say...? Can you really trust Him?'* And when they chose rebellion, sin entered the world like a virus. Darkness gained territory. The enemy smiled as God's children became slaves in his kingdom of darkness.

And we've felt the ripple effects ever since. Sin isn't just about bad choices – it's a power that corrupts everything it touches. It destroys relationships, twists desires, and breaks the world around us. Anger turns to violence. Greed robs the poor. Lust dehumanises others. Lies fracture trust. And underneath it all, the enemy whispers, 'This is freedom. Do what you want.' But in reality, it's slavery. Jesus said, *'Everyone who sins is a slave to sin'* (John 8:34).

That's the consequence of sin – not just the hurt and destruction we see in the world, but a deep separation from the God who made us. Cut off from His light, we are left stumbling in darkness, chained in a kingdom that only leads to death. So how do we know what sin is?

GOD'S HOLINESS IS THE MEASURE OF SINFULNESS

C.S. Lewis once wrote, 'A man does not call a line crooked unless he has some idea of a straight line.' He was pointing out that we can only recognise what is wrong when we know what is right. And what is 'right' is not determined by culture, opinion, or even comparison to others – it is measured against God Himself.

God is perfectly holy. The apostle John put it this way: *'God is light; in Him there is no darkness at all'* (1 John 1:5). Light is pure, complete, and powerful. By contrast, darkness is simply the absence of light. In the same way, sin is not some independent force – it is what happens when God's holiness is rejected, when His presence is pushed away. It is any deviation from God's standard of perfect holiness. That's why we symbolise sin with an 'X' in the Gospel Steps. Just as when you write a test and you get a wrong answer, instead of a tick, you get an X.

Here's where we can get it wrong. When we wonder if we're 'good enough,' our instinct is to compare ourselves to someone worse. We look at tyrants or murderers – Adolf Hitler comes to mind – and think, 'Well, I'm not as bad as him. Surely I must be okay.' But the Bible never invites us to measure ourselves against other people. Our measure is Jesus – God Himself, who became man and lived the life we were always meant to live.

When you look at Him, you see the straight line. You see the perfect standard of love, purity, truth, and holiness.

And against that standard, sin is revealed for what it really is: any deviation, any crookedness, any step away from God's holiness.

Knowing who God is – His holiness, His perfection – is what truly helps us understand what sin is. It's not simply about breaking rules; it's about breaking relationship with the God who is holy and loves us. What then is the consequence of our sin?

OUR NATURE IS CORRUPTED BY SIN

Sin doesn't just affect our choices; it affects who we are. The Bible explains that because of Adam and Eve's disobedience, we all inherit a corrupted nature. Paul wrote, *'All of us also lived among them at one time, gratifying the cravings of our flesh and following its desires and thoughts. Like the rest, we were by nature deserving of wrath'* (Ephesians 2:3).

This is why sin runs so deep. It isn't only about bad behaviour, it's about a broken nature. We are like branches cut off from the tree, trying to produce fruit but with no life flowing through us. Left to ourselves, we cannot make our way back to God. Our sin separates us from Him, because His holiness and our corrupted nature are utterly incompatible. It's like trying to blend oil and water. The two simply cannot mix.

Jesus referenced the kingdom of God by distinguishing between sheep and goats. In this context, the sheep represent those who belong to God's kingdom, while the goats symbolise those considered part of the kingdom of darkness. These are not merely good or bad sheep;

rather, they are beings of fundamentally different natures (Matthew 25:13-46).

This is the true tragedy of sin – not only that it harms us and others, but that it severs us from the God who made us for relationship with Himself. That separation leaves us restless, empty, and lost. As Isaiah wrote, *'Your iniquities have separated you from your God; your sins have hidden his face from you'* (Isaiah 59:2).

But the story of God does not stop with our separation. There is a solution.

JESUS DEFEATED SIN

When you were ***dead in your sins*** *and in the uncircumcision of your flesh, God* ***made you alive with Christ****. He forgave us all our sins, having* ***cancelled the charge*** *of our legal indebtedness, which stood against us and condemned us;* ***he has taken it away, nailing it to the cross****. And having* ***disarmed the powers and authorities****, he made a public spectacle of them,* ***triumphing over them by the cross.***

Colossians 2:13-15 (my emphasis)

From the very moment sin entered the world, God affirmed His rescue plan. He promised that one day, a deliverer would come – a child born into our story who would crush the serpent's head *'He will crush your head, and you will strike his heel'* (Genesis 3:15).

That promise was fulfilled in Jesus.

Jesus is unlike anyone else who ever lived. He didn't just teach about truth – He is the Truth. He didn't just point toward life – He is the Life. He didn't just talk about God – He is God, wrapped in flesh, walking among us (John 14:6). He lived the life we were meant to live, a life of perfect love, pure devotion and complete obedience to the Father. He is the 'straight line' Lewis spoke of – the measure against which all crookedness is exposed.

And then He did the unthinkable: He stepped into our place of judgment.

On the cross, Jesus carried the full weight of our sin and shame. He paid the debt we could never pay. His sacrifice on the cross broke the chains of sin and purchased our freedom. *'For the wages of sin is death, but the gift of God is eternal life in Christ Jesus our Lord'* (Romans 6:23).

And when He rose again three days later, He didn't just come back to life – He declared victory over death itself. The enemy out to destroy us who thought he had won was defeated. The gates of darkness were kicked open, and the Kingdom of God broke through.

That's the good news: sin no longer has the final word. Death no longer has the last laugh. The devil's claim over you has been cancelled. Jesus has opened the door into a whole new life.

When Jesus rose from the dead, He didn't just prove that He is God – He opened the door to a whole new reality. His resurrection is the dawn of new creation, and with it comes victory over sin, death, and God's enemy, the devil. The empty tomb is God's declaration that life wins.

This isn't just good news for the future; it's transformation for today. The prophet Isaiah had a vision of God on His throne. He saw angels crying out, 'Holy, holy, holy is the Lord Almighty; the whole earth is full of His glory.' (Isaiah 6:3). Isaiah was overwhelmed by the majesty and purity of it all, and he suddenly realised how small and flawed he was in comparison. That's the effect God's holiness has on us when we fully comprehend it - it opens our eyes to how different He is from us, completely perfect. God's holiness is the radiant beauty that defines every other attribute. To say that God is holy is to say He is set apart, infinitely above and beyond, in a category all His own. His holiness is dazzling light with no shadow, perfect love with no trace of selfishness, pure goodness with no hint of corruption. When we catch even the smallest glimpse of it, like Isaiah did, it shakes us to the core. Holiness is what makes God glorious, and yet it is also what makes His love for us so breathtaking - that the One who is so pure, so exalted, so utterly perfect, would choose to reach down to us.

The resurrection means, you are no longer defined by your past, by your failures, or even by your old nature, if you put your trust in Jesus. The offer is available to all to be restored and defined by what Jesus has done, rather than be defined by what they have done.

That's why Scripture speaks not just of forgiveness, but of new birth. Paul put it simply: *'If anyone is in Christ, the new creation has come: The old has gone, the new is here!'* (2 Corinthians 5:17).

Notice, it says *'if…'*. This word means two things. There is the possibility of victory and freedom over sin which offers hope, but also it is conditional meaning you need to choose. Three wonderful gifts are made available: you are welcomed into God's royal family, given citizenship in His Kingdom, and commissioned as His ambassador to the world.

FAMILY: You are no longer an orphan – you are a beloved son or daughter in God's family. Imagine a child in foster care, moving from house to house, never certain where they belong. Then one day, they're adopted into a loving home where the Father looks them in the eyes and says, *'You belong.'* That's what God does for us through Jesus: *'See what great love the Father has lavished on us, that we should be called children of God!'* (1 John 3:1).

CITIZENS: You are no longer a slave – you are a citizen of God's Kingdom. Think of someone living under a cruel regime, where fear and oppression rule every day. Then suddenly, they are granted citizenship in a land of freedom, justice, and peace. That's what Jesus gives us. *'Our citizenship is in heaven. And we eagerly await a Saviour from there, the Lord Jesus Christ'* (Philippians 3:20).

AMBASSADORS: You are no longer just surviving – you are an ambassador of the King. Picture an ambassador sent to a foreign land, representing their nation with dignity, entrusted with a message of peace. That's who you are now. You are sent into a broken world, carrying the message of reconciliation. Paul wrote, *'We are therefore Christ's ambassadors, as though God were making his appeal through us'* (2 Corinthians 5:20).

Family. Citizens. Ambassadors. These are not distant theological ideas. They are your new reality when you accept God's gift of eternal life. You receive these as gifts, then through you, God is able to make these gifts available to others.

CONCLUSION: THE DEBT IS CANCELLED AND THE ENEMY IS DEFEATED

In 1999, David Smith, a computer programmer, released a virus known as *Melissa* that spread like wildfire. It came hidden in an innocent-looking Word document and, once opened, infected over a million computers, causing more than $80 million in damage. Later, another programmer, Marcus Hutchins, created malware but was caught and redirected his talents to make significant contributions to cybersecurity.

Sin works like a computer virus. It was designed by a malicious enemy to corrupt and destroy what God had made good. When we give in to temptation to sin, we don't just get infected – we also become a channel through which the 'virus' spreads. We get it wrong, and we fail, like the X symbol indicates. As a result, we receive and transmit corruption and brokenness. But God's plan is greater. Think back to Troopa and his life before he encountered Jesus in contrast to him taking the gospel to the world as a mighty evangelist. Like a perfect judge, God deals with the guilt of sin. And like a loving Father, He transforms us, so that we stop spreading destruction and instead use our God-given gifts to bring life, goodness, and hope into the world.

This is what the cross and resurrection of Jesus have secured for those who will put their trust in Him. Their sin has been nailed to the cross. Their old life is buried, and they have been raised with Christ into newness of life, born again of God's Spirit. They are no longer a victim or carrier of sin's corruption – they are a child of God, a citizen of His Kingdom, and His Spirit lives in them.

They don't need to strive for victory – it has already been won. The cross symbol represents all Jesus accomplished through His life, death and bodily resurrection. The virus of sin has been disarmed. The debt is cancelled. The enemy is defeated. They are free.

And now, just as Marcus Hutchins turned from spreading harm to being part of the solution, we are all called to live as Christ's ambassadors – a living testimony that His restoring power is real.

Jesus has done it all.

How then can we access and apply what Jesus paid for? In the next chapter we will look at the magnitude of God's restoration plan.

CHAPTER EIGHT

STEP 3: THE MAGNITUDE OF RESTORATION

On April 15th 2019, the world watched in sorrow as flames engulfed Notre-Dame cathedral in Paris. The fire, sparked during ongoing restoration work, consumed the iconic wooden spire, much of the roof, and left the upper walls severely damaged. Though the altar and treasured rose windows were miraculously spared, the building stood wounded – charred, fragile, and surrounded by the lingering contamination of toxic dust and lead.

Yet, from the ashes, a vision of renewal emerged. Within days, efforts were underway to stabilise the cathedral and shield it from further harm. In 2020, plans were set in motion to restore Notre-Dame to its former splendour, using the same traditional techniques and materials that once raised it skyward centuries ago. More than 1200 skilled artisans, engineers, and craftspeople joined together, each one playing a part in reviving what had been lost.

With close to a billion dollars in donations (€846 million euros) from around the world, the restoration became a global testament to the value of what was broken and the hope that it could be made whole again. After nearly five years of painstaking work, Notre-Dame reopened on December 7th 2024 – its spire reaching once more toward heaven, a symbol of beauty restored.

The story of Notre-Dame is not just about stone and wood. It is a reflection, in miniature, of a far greater restoration already unfolding. In scripture, we are told of God's intention to heal what was broken in both humanity and creation itself – to restore all things through Christ.

The ruin and restoration of Notre-Dame cathedral has tremendous significance as we focus on the third step of our gospel message. Why? Because the New Testament writers refer to *us* as God's temple, meaning a place of His presence, a place of worship to glorify Him and honour His name. This is the vocation of mankind, as God's image bearers, but we fell short of His glory, and the temple was ruined. We were meant to live in perfect union with God and be like Him in this world. We were made to bear His light, His love, His rule, His Holiness, His goodness and kindness. Instead, we carry guilt, shame, hostility and depravity. Paul writing to the Corinthians said the following: *'Do you not know that your bodies **are temples of the Holy Spirit,** who is in you, whom you have received from God? You are not your own; you were **bought at a price**. Therefore, honour God with your bodies.'* (1 Corinthians 6:19-20, my emphasis).

When Paul states, *'...you were bought at a price.'*, he is referring to the significant cost of restoration. This cost is greater than any monetary value; it was the life of the Son of God. This statement is intended to convey the high value placed on individuals. To illustrate, consider the price difference between a regular family car and a Rolls Royce; the price tag indicates their respective values. Similarly, the ultimate price has been paid for the restoration of individuals and the world. Peter also stated: *'As you come to him, the living Stone – rejected by humans but chosen by God and precious to him – you also, like living stones, are being built into a spiritual house to be a holy priesthood, offering spiritual sacrifices acceptable to God through Jesus Christ'* (1 Peter 2:5).

All of creation – especially us – is meant to declare the glory of God. Through Jesus, God is restoring us, not just individually, but as living stones together. The introduction of sin had detrimental effects not only on individuals but also on relationships, families, and society. God is restoring society through Christian community. We were not made to exist in isolation but in unity and harmony with others. What good would one or even two stones be to the construction of the Notre-Dame Cathedral? It took many stones, carefully shaped and placed in connection with other stones to produce the magnificent building that expresses worship to God. As living stones, individuals are meant to be interconnected rather than isolated in their relationship with God. We belong together, built up as His spiritual house, where He can dwell.

Before we can be built up as a spiritual house, together with other believers, we first need to be restored individually. This starts with what the Bible calls repentance.

I MUST TURN FROM SIN AND TURN TO GOD

Repent *therefore and be* ***converted****, that your sins may be blotted out, so that times of* ***refreshing*** *may come from the* ***presence*** *of the Lord, and that He may send Jesus Christ, who was preached to you before, whom heaven must receive until the times of* ***restoration of all things,*** *which God has spoken by the mouth of all His holy prophets since the world began.*
Acts 3:19-21 NKJV (my emphasis).

Now, repentance is a word that sometimes feels heavy, even religious. But at its heart, repentance simply means this: turning. Turning from sin and turning to God. It's like being on the wrong train line, heading further and further in the wrong direction. The longer you sit, the more lost you become. But the moment you realise your error, you have a choice: get up, change direction, and start moving toward your true destination.

The u-turn symbol illustrates an arrow that first plunges downward before curving upward. Here, the Kingdom of God stands unmistakably above the arrow, while the Kingdom of darkness sits below. Remaining in sin, with a sinful nature, is not merely a passive state – it actively drives a person toward the kingdom of darkness.

Trusting in Jesus and embracing the reality of His death and resurrection enables true repentance, turning away from sin and directing one's life toward God. This shift is not just a change – it's a profound transformation, moving individuals from bondage under a tyrant to genuine freedom as sons and daughters of the King.

Repentance is not just regret. It's not self-help. It's not trying harder. It is recognising that only Jesus can save you and then turning to Him in trust. The moment you do, He meets you with grace, wipes away your sin, and begins His work of restoration in you. Grace is God's unmerited favour. His goodness poured out on us, received as a gift and something that cannot be earned. It is by grace that we are saved through faith as Ephesians 2:8 so clearly informs us. This is good news, as the price of our salvation is too great for us to be able to pay ourselves.

THE LOST SON RESTORED

The parable of the prodigal son in Luke 15 is onc of Jesus' most powerful stories. It tells of two brothers: the younger who rebels and is restored, and the older who resents his return - until the father lovingly appeals for him to welcome his brother back into the family. The story begins with the younger son demanding his inheritance from his father, leaving home, and wasting it all in reckless living. When a famine strikes, he finds himself broke, starving, and working among pigs - a place of utter humiliation for a Jewish man. Desperate, he decides to return home, confess his sin, and ask to be treated as a servant in his father's house.

But what happens next would have shocked everyone who first heard Jesus tell it. In a shame-and-honour culture, a son who squandered his inheritance like this would have been disowned forever. No respected patriarch would ever welcome him back, much less restore him. Yet Jesus' story turns everything upside down. The father sees his son from a distance, runs to him, embraces him, and kisses him before the son can even finish his apology.

This is God's heart revealed. The father doesn't just forgive; he restores. The robe, the ring, the sandals, the feast - each one is a symbol of sonship, dignity, and belonging. The ring in particular carried deep significance: it was a sign of authority, used to seal decisions and exercise ruling power. By giving it to his son, the father was saying, You are reinstated as my representative. You carry my authority again.

All the symbols declared: You are my child again. You belong in my house. You are restored.

That's what repentance is. It's coming to our senses, turning from sin, and discovering a Father whose arms are open wide - eager not only to forgive us, but to restore us.

I AM RESTORED TO RULE

So God created mankind in his own ***image****, in the* ***image*** *of God he created them; male and female he created them. God blessed them and said to them, 'Be fruitful and increase in number; fill the earth and* ***subdue*** *it.* ***Rule over*** *the fish in the sea and the birds in the sky and over every living creature that moves on the ground*
Genesis 1:27-28 (my emphasis).

God's restoration goes beyond just dealing with our sin. He doesn't just clean us up and put us on the shelf. As we see in Genesis 1, He restores us to our original calling: to rule as His image bearers.

In the Gospel Steps, we use two crown symbols to portray this. The big crown represents God as King over all creation. The small crown represents us – created in His image, designed to rule on His behalf. From the beginning, God blessed humanity and said: *'Fill the earth and subdue it. Rule over the fish in the sea and the birds in the sky and over every living creature that moves on the ground'*. We were meant to reflect the reign of God as King by stewarding His world with wisdom and care.

Sin robbed us of that role. We fell short of His glory and lost the authority we were created to carry. But listen to the apostle Paul's words: *'If, by the trespass of the one man, death reigned through that one man, how much more will those who receive God's abundant* ***provision of grace*** *and of the gift of righteousness* ***reign in life*** *through the one man, Jesus Christ!'* (Romans 5:17, my emphasis).

Did you catch that? Reign in life. That means God restores us to rule again – not as tyrants, but as His representatives.

The first time I entered the South African embassy in London, I saw the face of the great man, Nelson Mandela on the wall. He was the ruling president of South Africa at the time. Everyone in that building worked on behalf of their nation's authority. They spoke not with their own opinions, but with the authority of the one they represented.

That's who we are in Christ. Paul says, *'We are therefore Christ's ambassadors, as though God were making his appeal through us…'* (2 Corinthians 5:20). We are restored to represent the King of kings, to carry His presence into the world, to make His appeal through our lives and words.

So, restoration is not just about being saved from sin. It is being restored to reign – once again wearing the small crown, reflecting the glory of the One who wears the big crown.

CONCLUSION: FREED FROM SIN EMPOWERED WITH PURPOSE

This truth came home to me in the most unexpected way – through the loss of a young man named Luke.

Luke was the son of my childhood friend, Lee. At just twenty-one, he died suddenly in a car accident. He was kind, humble, gentle – a life full of promise cut short. Lee's grief was unimaginable.

But then something happened. While sorting through Luke's room in Wyoming, Lee opened a drawer and found a small Gideon's Bible. At the back, in Luke's handwriting, he made this discovery:

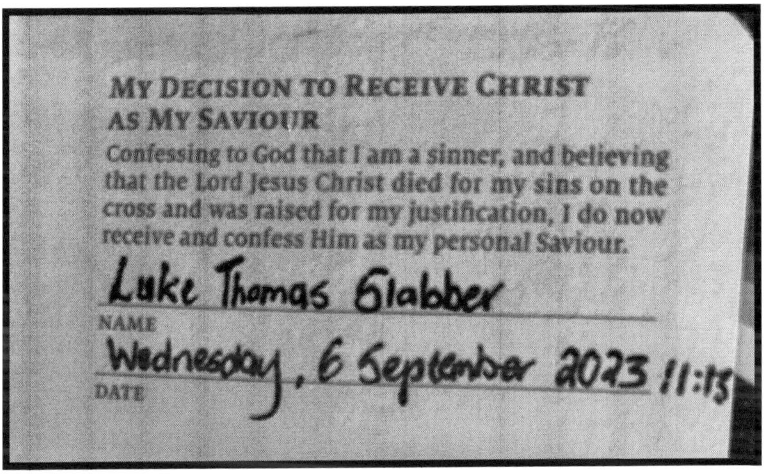

MY DECISION TO RECEIVE CHRIST AS MY SAVIOUR

Confessing to God that I am a sinner, and believing that the Lord Jesus Christ died for my sins on the cross and was raised for my justification, I do now receive and confess Him as my personal Saviour.

Luke Thomas Slabber

NAME

Wednesday, 6 September 2023 11:15

DATE

(used with permission from Lee Slabber, Luke's dad)

When Lee read those words, he describes a peace that came over him – not a peace that erased the pain, but one that carried him through it. He knew his son belonged to Jesus. He knew restoration had already begun in Luke's life, and that one day they would be reunited in the presence of God.

That is the power of the gospel. It restores us personally, building us into God's family, and one day it will restore all of creation when Jesus returns.

Like the Notre Dame Cathedral, God is at work to bring restoration to all that is broken through sin. He is not indifferent; God is love and God is King. The will and the way of the King is coming to earth as it is in the heavenly realm. He is looking for restored people, willing to respond to the call to be used by Him to help bring restoration where there is brokenness in the world. This is the magnitude of God's restoration:

- **God restores people individually** – forgiving sin, healing hearts, making us new.
- **God restores society collectively** – building us together into His spiritual house, a community that shines His light.
- **And one day, when Jesus returns, God will restore all of creation physically** – a new heaven and a new earth where He dwells with us forever.

Our message clarifies who God is and what He has done for us. The world is destined to once again be His dwelling place where He can live among us. What a glorious day that will be! Dallas Willard said the following about the gospel:

> The gospel that Jesus himself proclaimed, manifested, and taught was about more than his death for the forgiveness of our sins, as important as that is. It was about the Kingdom of God – God's immediate availability. There is so much more to our relationship with God than just his dealing with our guilt and sin. Once we have been forgiven, we are meant to live in the fullness of the life that Jesus came to give us.

We have work to do – work that involves putting on our shoes of readiness and heralding this glorious, good news. It involves receiving God's abundance of grace to rule according to the good works He has prepared for us, including sharing our faith.

To continue our journey with Jesus, of stepping into our calling as His witnesses, the next phase involves activating our willingness. There are three simple and accessible steps we can take to activate our willingness to proclaim the good news of Jesus Christ. You can do it! God wants you to take those steps, and you will be amazed at what He will accomplish through you when you do. In the next section we will look at these activation steps.

To see the Gospel Steps digital tract online, use the QR code above.

SECTION THREE

ACTIVATION

YOUR NOTES

CHAPTER NINE

PRAY : CULTIVATING GOD-DEPENDENCY

'How could he be so arrogant!'

The 2 to 3 a.m. slot on our volunteer patrol didn't bother me, because I had hoped being partnered with him would provide open doors for sharing the good news of Jesus.

We'd had many meaningful conversations, and some even about God, but that night he had crossed a line. Driving through the dark desolate streets for close on an hour, while straining my eyes to detect anything suspicious, added to my aggravation.

As I sneaked back into my house, trying not to wake the family, my angry thoughts led me to pray as I put my weary head on my pillow: 'God, I'm done praying for him.' I paused, then sulkily continued, 'I'm not praying for him anymore. I'm not trusting for gospel conversations with him. I commit him to you now. Amen!'

Not a very compassionate prayer, I know. Not one of my finest evangelistic moments. But somehow, I had convinced myself it was the right thing to do.

Still tired from the neighbourhood drive, I arrived at our church staff prayer meeting the next morning. With the rush of early rising, grabbing a coffee, and fighting the traffic, I had completely forgotten my prayer in the early hours of the morning. But God had not!

With about fifty people spread out across the room, praying in groups, I saw her bee-lining me. 'God just spoke to me Frans and said you must not stop praying for him.'

My heart sank as my frustrated prayer, just a few hours earlier came flashing back. Contrite, I asked God's forgiveness for my bitter heart, and for failing to recognise that prayer was making a difference, despite not seeing evident progress.

That moment taught me an enormous lesson about prayer and evangelism. The immediacy of God prompting someone to honestly rebuke me, got my attention. I had to repent of my heartless rebellion and for not trusting God with the results, and on top of that for abandoning a clear biblical instruction. Lastly, I repented for giving up on someone when God clearly had not. Since then, I've had several amazing conversations about God and the gospel with this man. I have seen his heart soften towards God and a growing curiosity about the Christian faith. While he has not yet made a commitment to follow Christ, I know God has not given up on him and nor have I. I am still praying for him many years later.

How active are you praying for people who do not know Christ?

Reinhard Bonnke, prominent German evangelist who preached the gospel to millions, transforming the spiritual landscape of a continent, said that 'evangelism without prayer is like a detonator without an explosive.'[1]

I like this. What good is a detonator without the power?

Charles Spurgeon, the great 19th century revivalist, stated that 'Prayer is the slender nerve that moves the muscle of omnipotence.'[2]

If we simply employ techniques and strategies and well-thought-out scripts for sharing our faith, we run the risk of being self-sufficient and missing what God can and wants to do through us for reaching the lost. We can either

be God dependent or self-sufficient, but we can't be both. Prayer is how we shift from one to the other.

I am not saying God can't or won't use you if you do not pray; He is so much bigger than that. If you are engaging the lost with the gospel, you're likely to be walking in the prayers of others. What I am saying is that you are called to participate in the prayer process for seeing lost people come to Christ and that prayer shifts us from self-sufficiency to God dependency.

PRAYER IS THE KEY TO REVIVAL

In his book, *Revival Rain*, my good friend Wayne Sandeman challenges us to pray for revival. He defines revival as God coming near, the church coming alive and the lost coming to Christ.[3] We need revival. We need the presence and power of God. We need to come alive through His presence. We need the lost drawn to God's presence in us. With amazing articulation, he describes what God did in past revivals, such as the Scottish Hebridean revival, the Welsh revival, and more. People repented on the streets, in the fields, in homes, without anyone preaching to them.

He outlines how these revivals were the product of prayer. He explains that revival is the answer to what we pray in the Lord's Prayer: *let 'your Kingdom come, your will be done, on earth as it is in heaven.'*

He challenges his readers with the following:

> Can we pray for this (revival)? Of course we can! The question is actually: Why haven't we prayed for this? Why has this not been our number one all-consuming prayer? Did we not know it's

> available? Did we not know it is possible? Or have we been too busy up until now? What have we been praying for? Is it really more important than revival? Could it be that we need reviving? [4]

This cuts me to the heart; busyness is the greatest barrier to my personal readiness. But I like how he encourages us to consider that maybe we need 'reviving' first. When we are revived, our hearts are filled with faith, passion, conviction and courage. We become renewed in our understanding and persuasion of just how magnificent God is and how desperately people need to know Him personally. We become filled with God's love for the lost and the conviction that the gospel can transform and restore them. We become revived as we pray. Revival flows to us, and then it flows through us.

Wayne offers a beautiful prayer that is repeated each day of his forty-day devotional on revival. It goes as follows:

> Lord, I bow my heart and bend my knee,
> Send revival, and start with me;
> Pour out your Spirit in an unprecedented way;
> May all who hear be saved today;
> May all who are saved proclaim the Way;
> Lord send revival and start with me.[5]

(If you want to know more about the forty-day devotional on revival you can visit the website www.40daysofprayingforrevival.com.)

If we pray for revival, we can expect a ready harvest. Let's consider a biblical view on prayer and evangelism.

BIBLICAL REASONS TO PRAY

The apostle Paul provides a profound process for engaging in gospel conversations. He encourages us to pray. He also encourages us to perceive and to proclaim, but I will speak of those in the following chapters. He emphasises prayer repeatedly. Prayer shifts us from self-sufficiency to God dependency. This is a critical shift for gospel fruitfulness.

> *Continue steadfastly in **prayer**, being **watchful** [perceive] in it with thanksgiving. At the same time, **pray** also for us, that God may **open to us a door** for the word, to **declare** [proclaim] the mystery of Christ, on account of which I am in prison— that I may make it clear, which is how I ought to **speak.***
> *Walk in wisdom toward outsiders, making the best use of the time. **Let your speech always be gracious**, seasoned with salt, so that you may know how you ought to answer each person.*
>
> Colossians 4:2-6 ESV (emphasis and parenthesis added)

Not only does Paul encourage us to pray, but he also instructs us to be watchful and thankful. If we believe God cares for the lost and listens to our prayers, shouldn't we be expectant for Him to respond? So, let's pray for the lost and then lift our eyes with expectancy to perceive what God is doing in response to our gospel-focused prayers.

Paul then instructs us to pray specifically for open doors so that he can declare, or proclaim the mystery of Christ, meaning the gospel. He asks for prayers of competence in proclamation, and finally he provides some instruction on how to proclaim: our rules of engagement. Namely, to be gracious and season our words with salt so that our listeners become thirsty for more.

Hebrews 4:12 speaks of the inherent power in the word of God, ready for the ingredient of our faith; and it is this power that moves the muscle of omnipotence. As we look at these significant texts, I pray they will stir your faith, raise your expectation, and activate you to pray as part of your preparation to proclaim.

I am operating off the assumption that we would not be instructed to pray for something unless it made a difference. I am also assuming that God's word produces faith in us, and that faith combined with prayer is powerful. Namely, we pray according to God's will when we pray according to His word; God responds to prayers that are prayed according to His will. With this in mind, let's dig into the incredible and powerful, world-shaking, fully-dependable Word of God.

PRAYER RELEASES LABOURERS INTO THE HARVEST

'Then he said to his disciples, 'The harvest is plentiful, but the workers are few. Ask the Lord of the harvest, therefore, to send out workers into his harvest field' (Matthew 9:37-38).

The harvest is ready! Jesus said it, not me. Maybe, more ready than we think. But the reality is, labourers are lacking. What do we do? We pray. Let's expect for God to hear our prayers and respond, that He will stir believers to grasp that they are more ready, the harvest is more ready, and that God is more willing to help than they may think!

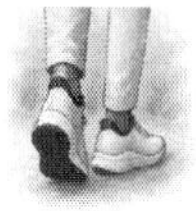

Let's believe for God to pour out His Spirit and, as Acts 1:8 says, that when the Spirit comes upon us that we will receive the power to be witnesses. Let's pray for this power to be released on new labourers as they go into the abundant harvest of lost souls.

PRAYER OPENS DOORS FOR THE GOSPEL

'Devote yourselves to prayer, being watchful and thankful. And pray for us, too, that God may ***open a door for our message****, so that we may proclaim the mystery of Christ, for which I am in chains'* (Colossians 4:2-3, my emphasis).

With a ready harvest, and labourers mobilised, what do we need next? Open doors! God opens the doors for the gospel. What is an open door? It's an opportunity to have a meaningful conversation about God with someone who is curious or aware of their need for God. They are open to hear about who God is and what He has done for them. Sometimes an open door is easy to spot, like if someone comments about your kindness, or comments that you are a peaceful person; they may even ask you directly about your faith or raise questions about God. Other times the clues to open doors may be more subtle, like when you notice a struggle in someone's life. Other times, God may speak to you directly about an open door that you may consider to be closed.

Remember when God spoke to Ananias about reaching out to Saul, the great persecutor of Christians at the time (Acts 9:10-16) Prayer is a divine partnership between God and us, where we get to participate in the process of God opening doors for the gospel. We need to do our part – pray – and then let God do His part to open doors.

'And even if our ***gospel is veiled****, it is veiled to those who are perishing.* ***The god of this age has blinded the minds of unbelievers****, so that they cannot see the light of the gospel that displays the glory of Christ, who is the image of God'* (2 Corinthians 4:3-4, my emphasis).

There is a hindrance to open doors that requires understanding and prayer focus. Based on 2 Corinthians 4, people are not only deceiving themselves or deceived by ideas around them: there is a spiritual enemy actively blinding, or veiling people from the truth. If we don't understand this reality, we may rely on natural means to defeat a spiritual enemy. We need spiritual weapons to defeat a spiritual enemy who is actively at work to keep people from responding to the gospel. These weapons are activated and exercised through prayer.

> *Finally,* ***be strong in the Lord and in his mighty power****.* Put on *the full armour of God, so that you can take your stand against the devil's schemes. For our struggle is not against flesh and blood, but against the rulers, against the authorities, against the powers of this dark world and against the* ***spiritual forces of evil in the heavenly realms****. Therefore* put on *the full armour of God, so that when the day of evil comes, you may be able to stand your ground, and after you have done everything, to stand.* Stand firm *then, with the belt of truth buckled around your waist, with the breastplate of righteousness in place, and with your feet fitted with the readiness that*

comes from the gospel of peace. In addition to all this, take up *the shield of faith, with which you can* ***extinguish all the flaming arrows of the evil one****.* Take *the helmet of salvation and the sword of the Spirit, which is the word of God.*

Ephesians 6:10-17 (my emphasis)

Notice the instructions to 'put on', 'stand firm', and 'take up' the parts of the armour and weaponry we need. We are in a spiritual war. God has provided weapons for the battles we face to reach the lost. But we are also expected to gear up and go; go to war against the spiritual forces opposing the advancing of the gospel! We do so through God's word activated through prayer and obedience. This connection between the spiritual weapons we have and the need to pray is made clear in the verses that follow immediately after the armour metaphor. Before we go there, let's consider:

the harvest is great; God is opening doors and because we are praying, we are defeating the enemy interfering with open doors. But what about us as the labourers? The remaining verses in Ephesians 6 give insights on how we as the labourers can raise our readiness and our effectiveness through prayer.

PRAYER PROVIDES COURAGE AND CLARITY

And pray in the Spirit on all occasions with all kinds of prayers and requests. With this in mind, be alert and always keep on praying for all the Lord's people. Pray also for me, that whenever I speak, ***words may be given*** *me so that I will fearlessly* ***make known the mystery of the***

> ***gospel**, for which I am an ambassador in chains. Pray that I may declare it **fearlessly**, as I should*
>
> Ephesians 6:18-20 (my emphasis)

We were on the streets of Douglas on the Isle of Man, with people recently trained in utilising TheGodTest to initiate gospel conversations, when I noticed how terrified Katy and Janet looked. I was suddenly concerned that they weren't ready, and silently prayed for them. Later, back in the comfort of the training centre, we offered our feedback. Katy and Janet were not the same women I had left on the streets hours before; they looked excited! They told us how scared they had been, but after taking time to pray, had experienced an incredible peace. Following that, they led three people to Christ!

Janet and Katy shifted from fearfulness to courage. Why? Because they prayed! How? By praying! God can do for you what He did for them. Whether it's the courage you need to initiate a spiritual conversation with a colleague, friend or family member, or whether you are participating in an outreach engaging strangers in gospel conversations, prayer is powerful to transform your heart and raise your readiness.

Colossians 4:4 states: *'Pray that I may proclaim it clearly, as I should.'* Have you considered that prayer could help you in a moment to know what to say? Often, when sharing the gospel, I have felt stuck, not knowing what to say. Then as I pray, I get a flash of inspiration that I know is the Holy Spirit responding to my prayer. It's interesting that in both the Ephesians and Colossians scriptures above, Paul states: *'...as I should.'* There is a standard of fearless declaration and clear proclamation that he

seeks to fulfil, and he seeks God's help to fulfil it through prayer. There are open doors around us, and we may even perceive them, but if we lack courage and clarity, we may never pursue them. Prayer provides courage and clarity.

PRAYER PROVIDES COMPETENCE

> *Such* ***confidence we have through Christ*** *before God. Not that we are competent in ourselves to claim anything for ourselves,* ***but our competence comes from God****. He has* ***made us competent as ministers of a new covenant****—not of the letter but of the Spirit; for the letter kills, but the Spirit gives life.*
>
> 2 Corinthians 3:4-6, (my emphasis)

> *On my account you will be brought before governors and kings as witnesses to them and to the Gentiles. But when they arrest you,* ***do not worry about what to say or how to say it. At that time, you will be given what to say****, for it will not be you speaking, but the Spirit of your Father speaking through you.*
>
> Matthew10:18-19 (my emphasis)

There are so many texts in the Bible where God promises to help us. We can pray with confidence and ask God, according to His will, to give us words to speak and to raise our competence beyond our natural ability as He provides supernatural ability. Worth repeating is God's promise of power to be His witnesses when the Holy Spirit comes upon us.

Then at Pentecost, it was when the disciples were gathered to pray that the Holy Spirit came upon them with power, and they went out on the streets proclaiming the gospel and three thousand new followers of Jesus were added on that day.

Acts 1:8

PRAYER POSITIONS US FOR INSTRUCTION

About noon the following day as they were on their journey and approaching the city, Peter went up on the roof to pray. He became hungry and wanted something to eat, and while the meal was being prepared, he fell into a trance. He saw heaven opened and something like a large sheet being let down to earth by its four corners. It contained all kinds of four-footed animals, as well as reptiles and birds. Then a voice told him, 'Get up, Peter. Kill and eat'.

Acts 10:9-13

Peter is praying; God speaks. What follows is a significant salvation of a Roman centurion, and a momentous theological shift in the minds of the early followers of Jesus.

And in Acts 8, I cannot help but wonder if Philip the evangelist was praying when he was visited by an angel and instructed to go to the road between Jerusalem and Gaza. The result was not just the Ethiopian eunuch coming to faith, but history tells us that it led to the gospel spreading to the region of Ethiopia and the surrounding areas.

I also wonder if perhaps Ananias was in prayer, when '*...the Lord called to him in a vision...*' (Acts 9:10-16). The result was Saul's conversion. It's like when I reached out to the two girls in Paris in the student dining hall. That open door would not have been perceived if I hadn't first prayed and received specific instruction to go to an empty table.

Prayer does not only release power for witnessing but is a means for God to instruct us in His mission when we give Him our attention in prayer.

HOW TO PRAY

There are amazing books and resources on prayer. One of my favourites is the Prayer Course by Pete Greig that uses the Lord's Prayer as an outline. (See www.prayercourse.org).

But if you are not in a daily habit of prayer, and don't know where to start, then here's a simple outline I've been taught that I have found very helpful. It uses the acronym ACTS: Adoration, Confession, Thanksgiving and Supplication.

I start by praying: 'Lord, I commit this time to you. Holy Spirit, I invite you to speak to my heart and guide me in my prayers. I'm here to listen and to obey. In Jesus' name.'

Then I proceed to the first focus as follows:

ADORATION

In this moment, I give God my full attention. My focus is not on my needs, nor on my circumstances, not even the needs of others. In this moment I focus on who God is, His nature, His character, His goodness. I begin to declare His goodness and His faithfulness in prayer.

For example, 'God, you are the creator of heaven and earth. You are loving. You are so kind and so generous. You are Jehovah Jireh.'

Draw from studying who God is as revealed in scripture and let that enrich this part of your prayer focus. No doubt you will find it drawing you closer to God as you fall more deeply in love with Him.

Then when I feel connected with God and aware of His incomparable nature I move onto the next focus.

CONFESSION

Considering God's glorious goodness, I become aware of my own sinfulness. I allow Him to shed His light in the dark places of my life. Sometimes they are very dark, other times it may be the subtlest of a shadow of compromise in my life. I consider people I need to forgive or people I may have wronged. I respond with repentance and receive His forgiveness and grace. This reminds me of the powerful gospel Jesus paid for with His own life.

For example: 'Father, I am so sorry for what I have done. I am sorry for... (I specify the sin) and for rebelling against you. Please forgive me. Holy Spirit help me to respond differently next time. I receive the cleansing blood of Jesus that washes me whiter than snow.'

When I know there is nothing bothering me in my conscience or spirit then I feel ready to move onto the next focus.

THANKSGIVING

Beginning with thanking God for His forgiveness and grace, I consider other areas of blessing in my life. I give God thanks, and I usually find my heart swells with gratitude and conviction that God is one who hears and answers my prayers. I try think of things I have prayed for previously where I've seen answers to prayer. For example: 'Father, thank you for your forgiveness. Thank you my sins are cast as far as the east is from the west. Thank you that righteousness is a gift received by grace. Lord, I thank you for my amazing family. (Then I mention specific things that are going well in the family) I thank you for your provision for... etc.'

By starting with focusing on God, then repenting, followed by thanking Him for His goodness, I find myself more ready for the last focus.

SUPPLICATION

Supplication is like making a request. With certainty in my heart of God's goodness and care, I can approach Him with things I would love for Him to take care of. Some of these are my own needs, or that of my family, others are the needs of people I know. They may also be of things I am reading about in the news. But one thing I pray for especially, is for revival and for the lost. For example: 'Father God, I want to pray for ...... (mention person by name), and their need for a job. I thank you that you have a plan and purpose for their life. Please would you guide them in your plans. Lord, I bring ... (person's name). I thank you for the conversation we had about you the other day. Please would you water the seeds that were sown in our conversation. Like Paul asked for prayer (Colossians 4), I'm asking you to please open another door for me to share the gospel with them...'

*

This is just one outline. I like the simplicity and the flow. But there are many other amazing outlines available.

Whatever your way of praying, my hope is that you will join me, Wayne and countless others, and pray for revival, asking God to start with you. Maybe you already are, and that is amazing! If not, I think God wants you to pray – to pray for people who don't know Jesus in your world, to pray for more labourers to go into the ready harvests around you, and to empower you as one of those labourers. What do you think?

Before we conclude our focus on prayer, there is another skill or competence worth cultivating for an effective prayer life; it is our ability to hear God.

HEARING GOD

If you reflect on previous chapters and the accounts I give of lives impacted with the gospel of Jesus Christ, so many of them involved prayer. I already mentioned the Paris example.

Edith, at our evangelism training, paused and prayed and asked God to show her people and places where she could share the gospel; God showed her a woman on the bus.

With Steve the big-wave surfer, he declined my offer to meet and chat after my first conversation with him. It was

two weeks later – after praying for him – that he asked me questions in the car park that led to him surrendering his life to Christ.

Katy and Janet conquered their terror through prayer and shared the gospel on the streets of Douglas.

When I was committed to stop praying for my night-patrol partner, God responded immediately with firm correction, reactivating me to pray for him.

HEARING STARTS WITH WAITING

Waiting and listening is important if we want to walk in intimate relationship with God. It shifts us from a monologue to a dialogue. It allows God to speak and not just be spoken to. None of us enjoy being around people who only talk about themselves the whole time. Eventually you start avoiding those kinds of people. While I don't think God will start avoiding you if you do not listen, I am persuaded that God wants you to listen so that He can impart, inspire and even instruct you according to His plans and purposes for you.

The last verse of Psalm 27 says the following: '*Wait for the Lord; be strong and take heart and wait for the Lord.*'

Prayer is how you can wait for the Lord, like the disciples did at Pentecost. Waiting for the Lord allows His active involvement in our prayer lives. But it starts by detaching ourselves from the clutter, pausing and giving God our fullest attention. It is not easy in today's clamorous world with so much noise and so much demanding our attention. But oh, so very necessary!

As we wait on God through prayer, it is an opportunity to hear from Him, which leads us to the second point.

Hearing and listening for His direction and instruction through prayer, will no doubt help raise your readiness, affect your willingness and enable more effective ministering of the gospel. Our world is filled with lots of noise. Many voices, many sounds, even what is occupying our thoughts can drown out hearing God's voice. Sometimes I frustrate my amazing wife Deb. She will share something with me and I will even say something in response, but the reality is I am thinking about something else at the time. From her perspective it seems like I am listening and hearing what she has to say, but I am not. It is as though she never said anything. We can do the same with God. Listen to the Holy Spirit. Give God your fullest attention in order to hear what He has to say. Listening produces hearing.

But maybe you are wondering, does the Holy Spirit still speak to us today? How can I hear God's voice?

A passage I found helpful is in 1 Corinthians 2. The apostle Paul is outlining how we minister the wisdom of God. He says the following, *'Eye has not seen, nor ear heard, nor have entered into the heart of man the things which God has prepared for those who love Him'* (verse 9 NKJV).

Now you could respond with, 'I knew it! We can't hear God directly. Paul confirms it.' Except, that is not where Paul ends; he goes on to say, 'But…'. This is an important but. He says, 'But God has revealed them to us through His Spirit. For the Spirit searches all things, yes, the deep things of God. For what man knows the things of man except the spirit of the man which is in him? Even so no

one knows the things of God except the Spirit of God' (verses 10-11).

Note what follows the word 'but': 'God has revealed them to us through His Spirit.' At this point you might still feel like God has all this knowledge that He keeps to Himself and is not revealing it to us, because Paul states '*Even so no one knows the things of God…*'

But here comes the punchline; are you ready for it?

'*Now we have received, not the spirit of the world, but the Spirit who is from God, that we might know the things that have been freely given to us by God*' (verse 13, my emphasis).

Wow! There you have it. We are born again with God's Spirit. God's Spirit is one with us and is the very means through which He can communicate with us. As we learn to wait on God and listen for His voice, we can grow in our ability to hear the beautiful and wonderful things He wants to say to us. Remember how Ananias heard from God to minister to Saul, who is the author of this book to the Corinthians? Do you remember Philip with the Ethiopian?

Paul goes on in the rest of this chapter and chapters following to teach and instruct on the function of the Holy Spirit in the lives of believers today.

CONCLUSION: PARTICIPATE WITH PRAYER

The world needs revival – God coming near, the church coming alive, the lost coming to Christ. According to my friend Wayne, every revival in history is preceded by prayer.

In John 17, we see the Lord's prayer. Not the Lord's prayer of Matthew 6 where Jesus instructed His disciples to pray. That is relevant too. But this is different. Here, it is a private moment between Jesus and His heavenly Father that the disciples had the privilege to observe. It begins with the request for the Father to glorify the Son. That is like praying for God to come near. He then talks to His heavenly Father about the authority He has been given, but for the purpose of giving eternal life as a gift to others. The definition of eternal life is also captured in this prayer – right relationship with Jesus and the Father. This speaks of the ministry of reconciliation, a call to proclamation.

He then intercedes for His followers, that includes you and me. He prays for our protection. Wow! He asks for us not to be taken out of the world but that we would be protected from the evil one while remaining in the world to finish His work. And then He changes gear in His prayer. In verse 18 He says, '*As you sent me into the world, I have sent them into the world.*' This is our commission. **We are to be like Jesus was in this world!**

Jesus proclaimed the message of the Kingdom and the way of salvation. He demonstrated the Kingdom by modelling ministry in the supernatural. He ministered with love and kindness, and He modelled and taught **prayer**! Then in verse 20 He states, '*My prayer is not for them [His followers] alone. I pray also for those who will believe in me through their message,*'. Jesus prayed for the harvest not yet reached. So can we.

The benefits of praying are enormous. It is not just a luxury; it is a necessity. When we take the time and pay the price, we receive courage, clarity and instruction, and we obtain competence and Holy Spirit power. Not only that, but labourers are released, doors open and the enemy is defeated! So, what are you waiting for? Give God your full

attention, listen carefully and hear what the Spirit of the Lord would say to you. Pray for the lost, lift your eyes with expectancy and perceive what God is doing in response to your gospel focused prayers. Raise your readiness to proclaim this glorious, good news through prayer.

*

In the following chapter we will look at the next step in actioning our willingness while wearing our shoes of readiness: the power of perceiving people.

YOUR NOTES

CHAPTER TEN

PERCEIVE: THE POWER OF PERCEIVING PEOPLE

Smith Wigglesworth was a powerful preacher who exhorted believers to be people of the Word and Spirit. He saw numerous miracles: crutches cast aside as God instantly restored broken limbs; cancerous tumours disappearing; blind eyes opened, and diseases healed. During his ministry, there were fourteen confirmed incidents of people raised from the dead.[1] Wigglesworth died in 1947, long before I was born, but David Griffiths knew him personally and he grew up with Smith, staying in his parents' home. You can imagine my excitement, when as a student I attended a seminar on the Holy Spirit with Griffiths, who had become a missionary to South Africa.

I sat riveted in these sessions as David shared powerful stories of lives healed and restored through the ministry of the Holy Spirit. He imparted faith, and profound truths from God's Word on the functioning of the Holy Spirit in the life of a believer. It was defining and radically changed my life. He not only taught, but he demonstrated what he taught.

Six years later, I was sitting at my desk in London, discouraged and disillusioned. I had just had an extremely tough time trying to minister the gospel to students on campus. In walked David Griffiths, smartly dressed and his white hair neatly combed. He walked over, fixing his gentle bright-blue eyes on me, and asked my name.

I should have felt nervous in the presence of someone who'd had such a profound impact on my life, but instead all I felt was an overwhelming peace and joy and a sense of, 'it's going to be okay.' That was not what I was feeling moments before, on the verge of tears of failure and frustration.

'My name is Frans.' I replied.

'Frans, what is your gift?'

I hesitated. I couldn't get myself to say it. Not after my terrible day on campus, but I did know the answer.

'You know your gift, what is it?'

Reluctantly I said, 'I am an evangelist.'

'You are right; you're an evangelist. But you are not an evangelist like Reinhard Bonnke or Billy Graham. You are ...' and he continued to do what the Bible calls prophesying: sharing with me supernatural knowledge God was revealing to him. He said: '... you are an evangelist with a pastor's heart and you will not bulldoze people into evangelism but you will shepherd God's people into the harvest to reach the lost.'

In that moment, it felt like Jesus was standing in front me, restoring my soul. I felt seen and understood, not just by David, but by Jesus. By looking me in the eyes, asking probing questions and with insight reflecting on who I am, he made me feel so very loved and seen. The much-needed joy and peace flowed to my parched and desert-dry soul. I was refreshed, restored, and inspired to not give up, but to persevere because God saw me; He loved me, and He understood.

What David did for me that day, is something you can do for others. People have a desperate need not just to be looked at or talked to, but to be *perceived* and seen:

to be seen for who they are, to be seen and understood. This is what it means to 'perceive'. The Merriam Webster dictionary defines *perceive* as:

1. To attain awareness or understanding of
2. To become aware of through the senses especially: see, observe[2]

Becoming aware of someone – to understand them and think about them – can have such meaningful impact. It is a gift that can be given, especially in today's 'smart phone' world where instead of seeing one another, what is most seen, is a small screen.

There is also another dimension of perceiving that can help us see and understand people like David Griffiths did with me. We can see people as God sees them, if we will cultivate the ability to hear His voice in a moment when we are in conversation with someone curious about the faith. We can see in the natural and then see in the supernatural as God enables us. More about that later.

OUR NEED TO BE SEEN

Have you ever observed two people talking while both are looking at a screen? We can get so lost in our digital world and forget what it is like to see or be seen. To give someone our fullest attention, to look and to listen, to reflect and then impart life to a weary soul is precious and beautiful, a dignifying gift to give.

Did you know that in psychology there is an area of study called *Person Perception Theory*? It examines why and how we try to understand people through sorting perceived information into mental categories and judging and responding accordingly.[3] We all tend to have lenses through which we see people. Sometimes these lenses cause us to filter certain people out so we don't see them at all; homeless people or service staff can fall into this category. Our lenses can create prejudice in us, meaning to prejudge. We treat others according to assumptions based on categories constructed in our minds. None of us like being filtered out or prejudged. All of us have a deep need in our souls to be seen and understood as we are, and when we feel that from someone, there is a connection made that is personal and powerful.

OUR NEED TO SEE

When we see people – really see them in their struggles, hurts, hopes, pain and pleasures – it gives opportunity for us to feel love for them. Whether they are broken or whole, God sees people as His image bearers, created for reflecting His glory in this world. We can see them in the same way, as He does. There is power in perceiving people and responding to them as God does.

Mark, in his Gospel, captures a moment when Jesus is conversing with a rich young ruler, and halfway through, Mark writes: '*Looking at him, Jesus felt a love for him...*' (Mark10:21).

Imagine that! I wonder if that rich young ruler felt what I felt when David looked at me? Sadly, the ruler walked away from Jesus, not willing to pay the price to follow Him. But Jesus gave him an eternal opportunity when He looked at him and felt love for him.

Jesus powerfully perceived people. Kenneth Bailey, a missionary for decades in the Middle East, attests to this in his book *Jesus Through Middle Eastern Eyes.* Here, Bailey helps us remove our modern cultural lenses so we can see in the same way the authors and readers in the Middle East would have at the time the Bible was written. In doing so, we can see more clearly and understand the message of God's word more accurately. Let's look and learn from his insights.[4]

SEE LIKE JESUS

One of the accounts Kenneth Bailey writes about is when Jesus wonderfully interacts with two people in the city of Jericho, captured in Luke 18 and 19: a blind man who is healed at the city gates, and Zacchaeus the wealthy tax collector. There is a risk of these two stories being disconnected, because the one appears at the end of chapter 18, and the other at the beginning of chapter 19, but as Bailey points out, this would not have been the understanding at the time since chapter divisions in the Bible as we know them, were not set by the authors. He highlights the connection between the two people: one is the oppressed, and the other, the oppressor. Jesus sees and cares for both. How amazing and wonderful is our Jesus!

Let's look at these two accounts.

SEEING THE OPPRESSED

> *As Jesus approached Jericho, a blind man was sitting by the roadside begging. When he heard*

the crowd going by, he asked what was happening. They told him, 'Jesus of Nazareth is passing by.' He called out, 'Jesus, Son of David, have mercy on me!'

Those who led the way rebuked him and told him to be quiet, but he shouted all the more, 'Son of David, have mercy on me!'

Jesus stopped and ordered the man to be brought to him. When he came near, Jesus asked him, 'What do you want me to do for you?'

'Lord, I want to see,' he replied.

Jesus said to him, 'Receive your sight; your faith has healed you.' Immediately he received his sight and followed Jesus, praising God. When all the people saw it, they also praised God.

Luke 18:35-43

The blind man saw Jesus, even though he did not have sight. Not physically, but he saw Him in terms of understanding who He was. He first refers to Him as '*Son of David*'; he sees Him as the rightful heir to the throne, a king. Then when Jesus asks what he wants from Him, he refers to Jesus as 'Lord'.

When people perceive Jesus for who He is – Lord and King – they are positioned to receive according to their perception. We can help people see the King who has the power to restore what is broken.

However, there were those who did not want the blind man to see Jesus. With hostility they try to shut him down. Jesus stops and has the man brought to him. While the text does not, on this occasion, state that Jesus looked at him and *saw* him, clearly He did.

Jesus makes no assumptions. He asks him a question. He interacts with him and gives him time to share his heart and desires. Wow! Part of seeing is *listening*. Not just looking but listening, not making assumptions but listening to a person's heart.

The blind man answers the question and states his need, and Jesus restores His sight. He and the people praise God as a result.

The blind man was a product of the systems of oppression. Because of his blindness he was relegated to begging for survival. In contrast, one of the most hated members of society at the time, were the tax collectors. They were Jews who aided the Romans in gathering taxes, and were entitled to exploit their fellow citizens, gaining wealth at their expense. They were considered part of the systems of oppression. Here's how Jesus interacts with a tax collector a short while after restoring this man's sight.

SEEING THE OPPRESSOR

> *Jesus entered Jericho and was passing through. A man was there by the name of Zacchaeus; he was a chief tax collector and was wealthy. He wanted to see who Jesus was, but because he was short, he could not see over the crowd. So he ran ahead and climbed a sycamore-fig tree to see him, since Jesus was coming that way.*
>
> *When Jesus reached the spot, he looked up and said to him, 'Zacchaeus, come down immediately. I must stay at your house today.' So he came down at once and welcomed him gladly.*

All the people saw this and began to mutter, 'He has gone to be the guest of a sinner.'
But Zacchaeus stood up and said to the Lord, 'Look, Lord! Here and now I give half of my possessions to the poor, and if I have cheated anybody out of anything, I will pay back four times the amount.'
Jesus said to him, 'Today salvation has come to this house, because this man, too, is a son of Abraham. For the Son of Man came to seek and to save the lost.'

Luke 19:1-10

Zacchaeus was a man who wanted to *see* Jesus, but his height hindered him. So, what does he do? He climbs a tree. He was a wealthy man, probably finely dressed. What would you think if you saw an adult, finely dressed, climbing a tree? But this man did not seem to care what people would think of him up in that tree. He wanted to see Jesus. What he probably did not expect, was for Jesus to see him, nestled between the leaves of the sycamore-fig tree. Not only does Jesus see him, but He wants to spend time with him. How amazing and wonderful is our Jesus!

Kenneth Bailey points out that those who were watching and seeing these events unfold would have been familiar with Ecclesiastes 4:1, and the connection here would not have been lost on them: 'Again I looked and saw all the oppression that was taking place under the sun: I saw the tears of the oppressed [the blind man] — and they have no comforter; power was on the side of their oppressors [Zacchaeus] — and they have no comforter.'

What a powerful insight from Kenneth Bailey, of a clear and compelling Kingdom being outworked. The will and the way of our King was established on earth as it is in heaven, with both the oppressed and the oppressor experiencing comfort and freedom. Why? Because Jesus looked, saw and reached out.

It can be so easy to overlook the needs of the rich and powerful in our society – those who seem to have everything, or not see the person who serves us at a coffee shop or restaurant, or the person on the street who stops to ask for money, or the shy work colleague who tucks themselves away behind a computer screen. Every person has needs. All are designed for relationship with God, their creator. Every living being needs Jesus. Let's see like Jesus.

THE CONSEQUENCE OF NOT SEEING LIKE JESUS

Jesus, the blind man and Zacchaeus were not the only people seeing that day. Luke captures the following: '*...all the people saw this and began to mutter*', referring to those who resented how Jesus treated Zacchaeus with kindness. They were not happy that this oppressor, who was already privileged, would now be further privileged by having Jesus in his home. What was Jesus playing at?

The results speak for themselves; because Jesus saw Zacchaeus – really saw him – He produced profound systemic transformation through this spiritually-hungry, broken individual. Zacchaeus repented and made restitution; he changed his ways and gave half his possessions to people like the blind man Jesus had just encountered.

We don't want to be like the people who saw and muttered, because then the oppressed and the oppressors would go unchanged. We want to be like Jesus who saw and cared. We as members of God's family, citizens of His Kingdom and ambassadors of the King in this world, can also be agents of transformation as we *see* people and proclaim the good news of our King.

How can we learn, and grow in our ability to see like Jesus?

HOW TO PERCEIVE

I was standing at the front of the line waiting for the doors to open, with popcorn in one hand and a drink in the other, when I noticed the extraordinary long nail on his baby finger. I was curious, so I struck up a conversation and eventually asked him about his fingernail.

He looked sheepish, and only after I asked a second time did he respond, still embarrassed, 'Actually it's for sniffing drugs.'

It wasn't the answer I was expecting. Doing my best to convey a sense of acceptance I responded casually: 'Have you been a drug user for long?'

I can't remember his exact response, but I do recall something about his several attempts to quit.

'Have you ever considered whether God may be able to help? Do you believe in God?' I asked.

'I do believe in God, but I've done too much wrong for him to accept me,' he replied with an edge of dejection in his voice.

'You may be surprised to find that you are exactly the kind of person he cares most deeply about. Would you

mind if I share with you who God is, and what he's done for us?'

About twenty minutes later we prayed together as he put his trust in the Jesus who saw him and cared for him, and cared enough to help me see and notice something as small, yet significant, as an extended fingernail.

How can we grow our competence to see people like Jesus saw them?

CULTIVATE CURIOSITY

Every person you meet has been created in the image of God. This means that their life has value and meaning. They are precious. Not only that, no two people who have walked the face of the earth are alike; every person is completely and utterly unique. Jesus thought us worth dying for. He said *'Greater love has no one than this, than to lay down one's life for his friends'* (John 15:13 NKJV). If God loves them, then who am I not to love them too?

If a person is completely unique, loved by God, and has intrinsic value and meaning, then why not live your life being curious about these precious image bearers of the creator of the universe? If it does not come naturally to you, then cultivate that curiosity. Take an interest.

I suspect Jesus enjoyed interacting with people because He deeply understood their value and uniqueness, and we can too.

LOOK FOR THE CLUES

As mentioned in the previous chapter on prayer, God is not willing that any should perish. I am persuaded that

God is at work wanting to save people and if we will allow ourselves to look carefully, we may find the clues to where He is working.

What helps me find those clues are two things:

1. Hurts
2. Hopes

Both relate to the heart. Seeing people becomes even more meaningful if we can see what is happening in their hearts. I heard someone once say that the heart is the organ of faith, and that faith is what is needed to be saved (Ephesians 2:8). Therefore, we need to speak to a person's heart. Matters of the heart can often provide the common ground needed for a meaningful rather than superficial conversation.

It is important to note, however, that while we may try to observe and hear what's going on in a person's heart, the Holy Spirit knows better what is really going on. In Luke 16:14-16 Jesus speaks of the Pharisees as being lovers of money; they put their hope in money. He states, '*You are those who justify yourselves before men,* **but God knows your hearts**, *but what is highly esteemed among men is an abomination in the sight of God.*' (My emphasis.)

1 Samuel 16:7 also makes clear that God looks at our hearts and knows their condition. The scripture is in the context of God directing Samuel in choosing the next king of Israel after the disastrous King Saul. The people had chosen Saul based on *external factors* such as his good looks, physical stature and strength, whereas David *from the outside* was a less likely choice.

Just as God knew the hearts of those Pharisees, and the heart of young David, chosen to be king, God knows the heart of every person we see.

Do you remember what Paul wrote in 1 Corinthians 2 mentioned in the previous chapter? Let me remind you: the Spirit of God searches the deep things of God and reveals them to us in our spirits. We have a communication channel with the all-knowing God. As we discuss briefly how to look for the clues, let's not forget this vital cooperation with the Holy Spirit, or else we risk relying on our own natural abilities.

(In the next chapter, *Proclaim*, I will share how to meaningfully relate the gospel to the hurts and hopes, and how to cooperate with the Holy Spirit in that as well.)

1. HURTS

Ask yourself, what are they struggling with? What is their deepest pain? While people may be protective of sharing their pain and their areas of vulnerability, clues are there. Think back to Steve with his alcohol abuse. Same goes with the guy with the long fingernail. It could be patterns of destructive behaviour, or a series of broken relationships that are observable. Facial expressions, body language and tone of voice can provide clues and insights regarding what is going on in a person's heart. God created a world that was originally only good; any hurt is a consequence of a world broken by sin, and the solution is the good news of God and His Kingdom.

Do you remember the two girls in Paris? They were struggling with loneliness and isolation. Even just hearing my accent brought them delight, let alone when God demonstrated supernaturally that He saw them in their struggle. In a similar way God ministered to me through David Griffiths. He brought a transformation to my weary soul after a frustrating day ministering on campus. God loves bringing healing, restoration, love and acceptance where sin, brokenness, frustration and weariness have brought destruction and pain. He wants to use you and me as His hands and feet in this broken world and reveal His love to broken lives.

2. HOPES

To find the hope-clues in their hearts you can ask yourself, what are they aspiring to? Or how are they trying to find meaning in their life? What are strongly held values or assumptions about what will help them thrive? It could be money, sex, drugs, alcohol, careers, relationships, success and the list goes on. Once again, how to follow these clues and steer them towards a meaningful gospel conversation will be covered in the next chapter, but here's a teaser: often those aspirations are a shadow of what they are made for, namely to be a member of God's family, a citizen of His Kingdom and an ambassador of the King.

Our purpose and meaning are fulfilled in a divine meaningful relationship with God, and by living out our vocation to reflect His glory and steward His creation. But the shadow cannot satisfy, only the cause of the shadow. That's where the gospel comes in.

*

Through seeing the clues of their hurts and hopes, whether by observation or divine revelation, we can minister the

good news of God to bring healing from pain and fulfilment of their created purpose.

CONCLUSION: IF YOU DON'T SEE THEM, HOW WILL YOU TELL THEM?

Let's go back to the moment after Jesus engaged the woman at the well, and reflect on what Jesus had to say about seeing (perceiving).

> *Don't you have a saying, 'It's still four months until harvest'? I tell you,* ***open your eyes and look*** *at the fields! They are* ***ripe for harvest.*** *Even now the one who reaps draws a wage and harvests a crop for eternal life, so that the sower and the reaper may be glad together. Thus the saying 'One sows and another reaps' is true.* ***I sent you to reap what you have not worked for.*** *Others have done the hard work, and you have* ***reaped the benefits*** *of their labour'*
>
> John 4:35-38 (my emphasis)

Jesus provided instruction to His disciples as He was preparing to gather those receptive individuals from Sychar. While the disciples were actively present during this period of harvest, they did not recognise its significance. Jesus further referenced labourers who sow without reaping, as well as those who reap where others have invested effort. Frequently, in my experience sharing the gospel, I have witnessed individuals make commitments to Christ, fully aware that numerous contributors had prepared them for that moment.

Some contributors, like the disciples at Sychar, may not have recognised the readiness of the harvest. This observation does not diminish the critical importance of those who sow and nurture, which has already been established. Nevertheless, it is equally essential to remain attentive to the opportunity to guide individuals towards making definitive decisions for Christ. As Jesus instructed His disciples, *'...open your eyes and look at the fields!'* Without deliberate attention, opportunities may be overlooked, and the potential for reaping may be lost.

I met with Scott McNamara, an evangelist known for developing the *Jesus At the Door* resources. During our conversation, he shared a significant moment in his ministry when he learned that 96% of Christians are not actively leading others to Christ. This realisation led him to conclude that while many believers either sow or water seeds – or do not participate at all – few focus on the act of reaping. Citing scripture from John 4, he described how this insight motivated him to dedicate his efforts to reaping. Since adopting this approach, he has played a pivotal role in equipping and mobilising believers across more than thirty nations, resulting in substantial impact.

To reap, we must first see. By looking with guidance from the Holy Spirit, we can recognise people's hopes and struggles, whether they are oppressed like the blind man at Jericho, or an oppressor like Zaccheus, in need of freedom from greed. God wants to use you; He wants to send you to gather where you and others have laboured.

How do you activate your reaping? It helps to have a clear and simple strategy for beginning and guiding conversations that lead to proclamation.

CHAPTER ELEVEN

PROCLAIM: A SIMPLE STRATEGY

If only I had made a different decision. The details escape me, but what is vividly etched into my memory, is the doorway at the end of a series of archways, beckoning me to enter. These were not the archways of the bitterly cold and dark Paris campus I mentioned earlier; this time the beckoning door was at the end of Trousdale Parkway – a walkway in the much warmer climate of California.

It was the end of the day during my campus ministry internship at the esteemed University of Southern California (USC). As I was approaching the exit to the university, I spotted the sign pointing to the School of Philosophy. I felt a nudge to enter the door that had unexpectedly grabbed my attention. Instead, I looked at my watch and rushed off to my next, insignificant destination.

Years later, while watching a video of famed author, philosopher and theologian, Dallas Willard, I discovered that he had been a lecturer, professor and eventually department head at the USC School of Philosophy. He had served there for forty-eight years, including the year of my internship. As I heard this, my heart sank as that moment at USC, years earlier, came flashing back. Was it the Holy Spirit nudging me that day? Had God wanted to gift me with an opportunity to meet this most remarkable thought leader?

I will never know, because instead of following the nudge and seizing the opportunity, I chose to ignore the door.

Have you ever missed a door of opportunity?

Remember Colossians 4? Paul asked believers to pray for him that God would open a *door* for the gospel. Prayer can prepare the doors of people's hearts to open to God and let Him into their lives. Through prayer, God can also lead you to doors that are already open. Paul also asked for prayer so that he would *proclaim the gospel* clearly.

Praying helps open doors. *Perceiving* helps you see the doors God is opening. But if all you do is pray and perceive and you never *proclaim,* you'll miss the opportunities God has for you. Missing an opportunity to meet a profound thought leader is one thing, but missing an opportunity to alter an eternal destiny and save a soul from relational separation from God is a different thing entirely.

Have you ever come across the statement, 'Preach the gospel and if necessary, use words?' I like the response of famed missiologist, Ed Stetzer. He wrote an article titled: 'Preach the Gospel, and since it's necessary, use words.' [1]

While it is true that our actions need to reflect the message we proclaim, being kind and loving and caring for people is just not enough. It does not replace the need to still clearly proclaim the amazing message of Jesus and His Kingdom if people are going to choose to follow Him.

After all, as Romans 10:14 points out: 'How, then, can they call on the one they have not believed in? And how can they believe in the one of whom they have not heard? And how can they hear without someone preaching to them?'

Part of our willingness needs to be to take the risk and step through the open doors for the gospel that God puts before us.

As Deb and I have trained and mobilised countless people to fruitfully engage the lost, we have noticed that often the biggest hurdle is bridging the gap between perceiving and proclaiming.

Deb uses a great illustration for this. Have you ever seen the famous Tower Bridge in London? It's an enormous blue and white drawbridge. She uses a small Lego model to demonstrate the point. The drawbridge has two sides that get raised or lowered depending on the need for large ships to pass under it. She explains that when it comes to ministering the gospel, we need to lower our side of the conversational bridge. That is the process of praying, perceiving and then initiating an intentional conversation. If we do a good job of it, then they should hopefully respond by lowering their side of the bridge. She has a little Lego model of a red London bus that represents the gospel. For the gospel to reach their hearts both sides need to lower their part of the bridge, starting with us.

In this chapter I will be outlining a strategy for helping you lower your side of the bridge in a way that provides the best chance of getting them to lower their side. It is for finding and entering the doors God leads you to. This is what we call the SALT strategy.

THE SALT STRATEGY FOR OPEN DOORS

In Colossians 4:6, Paul instructs that our conversations need to be full of grace, *'seasoned with salt'*, so that you may know how to answer everyone.

What does Paul mean by *'seasoned with salt'*? Have you ever eaten a very salty snack? There's a reason why bars often give salty snacks for free. They leave you thirsty, needing more drinks.

Jesus said, *'Let anyone who is thirsty come to me and drink. Whoever believes in me, as Scripture has said, rivers of living water will flow from within them'* (John 7:37, 38).

There is a way you can have conversations with people that can cause them to thirst for the rivers of living water available through Jesus. There are also ways you can engage that will burn bridges and turn people away.

How can we have salty conversations? Dr Rice Broocks came up with the very simple strategy captured by the appropriately named acronym, SALT. Easy to remember and profound in its use, it is a good approach to either reveal an open door or help unlock a closed one. It stands for:

Start a conversation
Ask questions
Listen
Tell the story

Many conversational evangelism approaches involve starting a conversation then jumping straight to telling the story. This can be like walking into a glass door; you will bang your head and cause pain. This approach may work with someone very ready to make a commitment, but not everyone we meet is ready. In fact, in most contexts, most people are not ready. It risks making a person feel badgered if we try force the gospel on them. It is far more constructive to first ask questions, gain understanding through careful listening, then respond appropriately based on what you discover. It is interesting that Jesus

often engaged people through questions, especially seekers and sceptics.

So, let's unpack the SALT strategy.

START A CONVERSATION

We have conversations all the time. A SALT conversation is one where there is intention to steer it towards a meaningful conversation about God, and then the gospel if appropriate. Starting a SALT conversation can be with anyone: it could be with a stranger, a work colleague, a friend, a family member, a neighbour or someone else. Whoever they are, look for something of interest, or something you might have in common with which to start a conversation. Finding common ground can help ease into a conversation. For example, when I was surfing regularly, it was the most natural thing to arrive on the beach and ask another surfer I had never met about the surf conditions. This first step is just about getting a conversation going. Anything goes. It is a general conversation starter to make a connection.

Deb is amazing at this. She very naturally will find something to either comment on or ask a question about. She will start a conversation asking about what someone is wearing, or by commenting on their children's good behaviour, or she may sympathise with an obvious challenge. Conversations can also be started through observing a need and offering to help. The focus is general at first, because once a conversation is started you can steer it from general topics to God, and then to the gospel.

Why not give it a go? Initially the conversations you start don't need to lead to a God or gospel conversation;

it's a baby step towards cultivating a lifestyle of initiating gospel conversations in a way that is natural. It may be challenging to begin with, but the more you do it the more confident you will become.

ASK QUESTIONS

The goal of asking questions in a conversation is to avoid a monologue and create dialogue. It helps build trust and a relational connection while offering opportunities for ministering the gospel. Good questions can steer conversations, gently challenge strongly held assumptions, and they can also guide people to discover truth for themselves, rather than being told what is true.

The following types of questions may be useful:

1. Questions for showing interest
2. Questions to discover common ground
3. Diagnostic questions
4. Steering questions
5. Permission questions
6. Questions to help them discover truth

Let me unpack these a little.

QUESTIONS OF INTEREST

Questions of interest are the most general. At this point be curious. Cultivate curiosity about this precious, unique person created in God's image and who He loves exceedingly. Take an interest in who they are, what they

enjoy, what they think of the world and themselves. There are countless areas that can be explored about a person's life.

COMMON-GROUND QUESTIONS

This means looking for areas of common interest that can help make a connection. People enjoy exchanging insights and perspectives with people who have the same interests. Having a conversation unrelated to God helps establish a relational connection that also deepens a sense of trust. Later when you start speaking about God or the gospel, they may be more inclined to hear what you have to say because you took time to discuss other areas of interest.

DIAGNOSTIC QUESTIONS

Diagnostic questions help you discover what is going on in a person's heart in the same way a doctor asks questions of a patient to learn about their symptoms. This helps them pinpoint what's wrong and prescribe a remedy.

Diagnostic questions help us discover what they believe. They can also help us discover what the hurts or hopes are in their hearts, as we discussed in the previous chapter. These insights can help you find the open doors for ministering the gospel. It can help you gain insights for where the gospel connects with their felt need. But even if you don't discover hurts or hopes, like with common-ground discussions, taking an interest in what they are interested in can also establish a relational connection and build trust.

STEERING QUESTIONS

A good steering question will relate to what you are already discussing but it shifts the conversation in a different direction. For example, a question I often ask when a person has opened up about a struggle, is: 'Have you ever considered if God could make a difference in that area?' Or if we have discussed something more philosophical, such as moral issues or issues related to meaning in life, I ask, 'Have you ever considered what the Bible has to say about this topic?'

If we have talked about a variety of topics and it seems appropriate to offer another topic, I'll ask something like: 'This is so interesting chatting about these things. I find your perspectives interesting. Here's something I'm curious about, are you interested in spiritual things at all?' If they say yes, then the conversation can naturally open to talk about God. If they say no, then I'll ask them why not.

PERMISSION QUESTIONS

If we are already talking about God or spiritual things and I want to steer the conversation towards the gospel, I'll ask something like, 'Has anyone ever explained to you who God is and what he's done for us?' If they say no, I don't assume they want me to. Then I will ask what I call a permission question, 'Would you like me to?'

By asking permission I'm engaging their willingness to listen rather than forcing my views when they may not be interested. If they say no, I respect their wishes and usually I'll change the subject. It means this is not a door that God is opening for me right now. Occasionally I will sense an

unction from the Spirit to probe deeper as to why they would rather not, then I do so respectfully and sensitively.

QUESTIONS TO HELP DISCOVER TRUTH

What about guiding someone to the truth through a question? Sceptics that Jesus often had to deal with were the religious leaders, the Pharisees being one group. Matthew 22:41-45 captures this account: *'While the Pharisees were gathered, Jesus asked them, "What do you think about the Messiah? Whose son, is he?"'* (verse 42).

Jesus is getting them to think about their point of view and is leading them to a topic for a truth discovery.

'"The son of David," they replied.' Jesus was expecting this answer from them. He had asked them a guiding question because he already had insights about their beliefs. If I'm engaging a secular materialist, the questions I ask will be different to the ones I pose to a Muslim or someone deeply interested in Eastern mysticism.

These types of questions anticipate an answer based on what you've gathered about their point of view.

Jesus continues, *'How is it then that David, speaking by the Spirit, calls him "Lord"? For he says, "'The Lord said to my Lord: 'Sit at my right hand until I put your enemies under your feet.'"'* Then comes the punchline from Jesus, *'If then David calls him "Lord", how can he be his son?"'* (verses 43-45).

Jesus was challenging their assumptions about the Messiah to guide them to the truth through a series of questions. This was a better approach than getting into an argument and just telling them that they were wrong and forcing the truth on them.

Thinking of questions to ask may come more naturally to some people than others. That's okay, but it is a skill you can grow in.

LISTEN

Listening is more than just being quiet while someone speaks. Most people don't listen with the intent to understand, they listen with the intent to reply. We need to make the effort to listen well, and while they are speaking, to restrain ourselves from constructing a persuasive argument in our heads to prove our point while disproving theirs. This posture burns bridges and builds barriers, instead of the other way round.

You want to seek to understand the person you are speaking to. Be curious. Who are they? What are they all about? What are the hurts they are carrying? What are the hopes and dreams of their hearts? Where are they trying to find meaning in their lives and how is that working for them? What makes them come alive? What you ultimately want to listen for, and discover, is what God is doing in their life.

There are skills you can develop to be a good listener. Here are some tips to get you started:

1. Reflect to them what they are saying in your own words.
2. Ask questions about what they are saying.
3. If something they say isn't clear, ask clarifying questions.
4. Make eye contact.
5. Don't interrupt.

6. Concentrate on what they are saying; don't think about other things.
7. Pay attention to non-verbal cues such as tone of voice and body language. This helps indicate what is important to them or what agitates them etc.
8. If you sense they are getting agitated, gently enquire about your observation.
9. Don't criticise; rather listen for what you can encourage.
10. Be aware of your own non-verbal communication and the message you are sending.

Listening to someone is a gift we can give. Taking the time and making the effort to listen well can make someone feel heard. Feeling heard opens hearts. I have had many experiences asking questions and listening to responses, and then asking more questions and listening some more, until eventually I am asked: 'So what do you believe?' I find when this happens, they are more receptive than if I had tried to push my beliefs on them to begin with. If you really struggle with listening, there are plenty of YouTube videos that can help.

If you regularly pray, perceive, start conversations, ask questions and listen well, then you will find open doors for ministering the gospel. This is when you get to tell the story.

TELL THE STORY

How magnificent! You get to tell the story of God's existence, and how, despite the terrible state of our world and the brokenness of our human condition, God has an incredible plan of restoration. This is where you share that we are made for relationship with God, that He loves us and has a plan and purpose for us, but it's our sin that separates us from Him. You get to tell them that God made a way through Jesus for us to be restored in right relationship with Him, and not only that, but should they choose to become part of His holy family, they can become citizens and ambassadors of His heavenly Kingdom, which is accessible now. And best of all it is a gift; it's free for us, but it cost God dearly to pay the debt of our sin in the sacrifice of His son, Jesus.

When presenting the good news of Jesus, we should be clear, concise and personal. We want to share it in a way that is *salty.* Ensure you, as the messenger, represent the message in how you present it. Being kind and respectful is likely to leave them wanting to know more, whereas if you are argumentative and judgemental you will achieve the opposite. Here are some tips.

1. FOCUS ON JESUS

- Jesus is central to the gospel so make Jesus the focus rather than getting sidetracked by other doctrinal issues.
- Present Jesus like you are introducing them to your best friend. Share your own story of how you met Jesus and the difference He's made in your life.
- Share Jesus enthusiastically and with conviction.

2. USE THE WORD OF GOD

- Unless circumstances don't allow for it, try share with them from the Bible. It starts the discipleship

process even before they are a follower of Jesus. Sharing from the Word enables the Holy Spirit to convict them of its truth.

- Before presenting the Bible verses, ask if they are okay reading from the Bible.
- Still share from the Bible even if they don't believe it is true. There is inherent power in God's Word even if someone does not believe it.
- It helps to be able to answer questions about the reliability and credibility of the Bible, but avoid getting bogged down in details if it is not a deal breaker to them.

3. MINISTER THE GOSPEL

- Minister, don't just give information. You minister by relating the gospel to them personally and compassionately. Their hurts and hopes give opportunity for personalising the gospel. By doing this you are ministering to the heart and not just speaking to the head.
- If you can identify with their hurts and hopes, share your experience of how Jesus made a difference in those areas.
- Listen to the Holy Spirit and be ready to minister with God's supernatural ability. God knows people's lives in detail and can share this with you through the Holy Spirit – using thoughts, images, Bible verses, or stories.
- Offer to minister to them through prayer for specific needs, including needs for healing miracles. Some individuals may prefer not to receive prayers

immediately, however, if they are open to it, it can provide an opportunity for a personal experience of God.

4. CLARIFY THE DECISION

- Faith in Jesus is a decision of the will; make the choice clear allowing them to respond with a clear yes or no to the invitation to follow Christ.
- Think of the parable of the pearl of great price: a merchant, who recognised the value of a single pearl, sold all he had to purchase it. When they have grasped the beauty of the gospel, they will be ready to be presented with the decision to 'sell all' to attain it.
- If they carefully consider the commitment and sacrifice it takes to follow Christ before deciding, they are more likely to follow through with their decision.
- When you have presented the decision, give them a moment to consider it; be quiet and don't interrupt them. This is a moment for God to speak to them, not you.
- While they are contemplating the decision, silently pray for them. There is a war raging for their soul.

*

By now I trust you've grasped the simplicity and the profoundness of the SALT strategy for conversational evangelism. When done with a loving posture and genuine care, it is so insightful and helpful. I really hope you give it a good go and find it beneficial.

A person's readiness will determine their responsiveness. Let's consider the responses you can anticipate, and how you can make the most of the moment.

FOUR TYPES OF PEOPLE

The apostle Paul gives insight to the fact that people are at different places of readiness, and that the journey to salvation may be a process. See what he says here in 1 Corinthians 3:6-7:*'I **planted** the seed, Apollos **watered** it, but God has been making it **grow**. So neither the one who plants nor the one who waters is anything, but only God, who makes things grow.'* (My emphasis.)

Can you see how different people at different times may contribute differently to someone's faith journey? Sometimes we are sowing the Word of God in the soil of people's hearts. Other times we are watering what has been previously sown. God is the one who makes things grow, meaning the truth of the Word starts impacting their hearts. We can expect opportunities to also reap what others have sown through prayer, relational investment, and ministering the gospel. Note there are different roles here. There is our role and then there is God's role. Our role is to pray, perceive, sow and water. God's role is to open doors and make the Word grow. Our role then is to minister the gospel (proclaim) and clearly present the decision they need to make. Then finally their role is to respond with a decision. Sometimes people wait for God to do what we are meant to do and try do what God is meant to do.

You may have come across the Engel Scale, developed by James F. Engel and published in 1975 in his book, *What's*

Gone Wrong With the Harvest? It's a way of describing a person's journey of faith from no knowledge of God to full maturity. A minus ten represents no knowledge, a plus ten represents a fully mature follower of Jesus and zero is the point of decision to follow Christ.

In our training we have adapted the Engel Scale[2], drawing on insights from Nick Pollard in his book, *Evangelism Made Slightly Less Difficult* (some may feel this title is not optimistic enough, but it was written in a Western secular context when there was a lot more cultural animosity towards the Christian faith). Below is a table that describes four types of people you are likely to encounter. The first column positions them on the Engel Scale. The second column describes their attitude to the gospel. The third column describes our focus in the conversation as we ask questions, listen and dialogue.

POSITION	POSTURE	FOCUS
-10 to -8	Anti-God	Pebble in the shoe
-7 to -5	Indifferent	Stir interest
-3 to -2	Interested	Identify & deconstruct obstacles
-1 to 0	Ready	Minister the gospel & help them decide

ANTI-GOD

If you meet someone who is anti-God, sharing the gospel with them may well make them even more anti. That doesn't mean you cannot help them.

I had a conversation with a professor, seated next to me on a plane, who was an intellectual atheist. He kept saying he wasn't a person of faith but a person of science as if the

two were mutually exclusive. I explained that Deb was a biologist and a Christian, but he struggled to accept this. I described a hypothetical example of a miracle and asked if that happened if he would consider the possibility that this could be evidence for God. His response surprised me: 'Absolutely not, science would have an explanation.'

I gently pointed out to him that he was also a person of faith, and that his faith just happened to be in science and not God. To his credit, he recognised this was true, and was shocked and appalled at himself for also being a person of faith.

Do you want to know what he did next? For the first time in the hour-long conversation, he asked a question: 'You said your wife was a scientist and yet believes in God, how does she reconcile the two?'

My focus in this conversation was not to try share the gospel with him. My focus was to put the proverbial pebble in the shoe. I was hoping to ask a question or make a point that would cause him to doubt his certainty that God does not exist. I had a strong sense that was achieved.

When it comes to a person who is 'anti-God' (a -10 to -8 on the Engel Scale), there is a journey and process usually needed to help them come to the place of being 'ready'. A *pebble in the shoe* helps them become interested; that is a win! Remember, God is at work, and salvation is a work of the Spirit. Our contribution helps shift them along the journey so that the next person who has a God conversation with them may find them closer to the point of readiness.

Worth noting is that people usually have a reason for not believing in God. It can be very worthwhile probing gently into why they don't believe in God or why they are so hostile.

INDIFFERENT

Someone indifferent is not bothered about issues of faith. They may have compartmentalised the subject, tucked it away somewhere with no interest in giving it much thought. Here, the focus is on creating interest.

Asking questions and listening carefully to their hopes and dreams may help. You may find something interesting to share about the Christian faith that they may not have considered that relates to hurts or hopes in their hearts. For example, someone very spiritual may be surprised to find out how much the Bible has to say about the supernatural. It also helps to gently challenge false perceptions they have about the Christian faith. For instance, individuals who view the Bible as outdated, might perceive God as irrelevant to contemporary life. Alternatively, they may believe that God is indifferent, remote, and inaccessible, making the pursuit of faith seem unwarranted. Some may view God as a tyrannical figure or a harsh judge, often stemming from negative encounters with authority figures. These perspectives, among others, while not provoking hostility, may result in an overall disinterest in exploring the Christian faith.

How do you gently challenge these and other false perceptions? Restating their perceived viewpoint and following up with a probing question may encourage a shift from indifference to interest in a gentle manner. For instance: 'When you mentioned..., it appears that your perception of God is... Have you ever studied the life of

Jesus and his interactions with people? Do you think he embodies that perception?'

With someone indifferent you will want to see them shift from indifference to openness and curiosity before presenting the gospel to them.

I met someone on a bus, and we later had lunch to continue our conversation. He was interested in spirituality, tarot cards, and Eastern mysticism, but not Christianity. He wasn't hostile, just indifferent. When he shared some unsettling supernatural experiences, I asked if he had considered seeking help from God. This began a friendship and exploration of faith that eventually led him to commit his life to Christ.

Another example is when I encountered a student on campus who aspired to a successful career but was struggling academically due to a lifestyle focused on partying and hedonism. At that time, he had no interest in Christianity. I approached the situation carefully, ensuring not to convey any personal motives or idolise his career ambitions, while guiding him towards understanding that Jesus has a plan and purpose for his life. By emphasising the harmful effects of sin and our need for Jesus as a Saviour, I was able to engage in a meaningful conversation about the gospel, which ultimately led to his decision to commit to following Christ. His aspirations, while being selfish, triggered a meaningful gospel conversation that challenged his indifference about the Christian faith.

Identify the common ground between their beliefs and the gospel, then help them see the connection. This can turn indifference into interest.

Imagine meeting someone who has questions about the Christian faith. They are curious, possibly due to a credible Christian influence, a praying relative, or something seen on social media. The Holy Spirit utilises numerous impactful ways to influence the lives of individuals who have not yet come to know Jesus. You get to be the person to help them figure out the barrier they have for committing their life to Christ, and with God's help, you get to help them overcome that barrier. Wow! What a privilege.

It is not uncommon for individuals who are curious about Christianity, or even considering becoming Christians, to encounter obstacles that prevent them from making a commitment to follow Christ. These barriers may involve questions regarding faith and science, issues surrounding evil and suffering, or a strong attachment to their current lifestyle.

You may wonder whether you are equipped to address such barriers. It is likely you will face this challenge at some point. It is important to remember that God cares deeply for each person and has been actively working in their lives prior to your conversation. God can speak to you and reveal unexpected insight or analogies; this is what the Bible refers to as *'words of knowledge'* or *'words of wisdom'* (1 Corinthians 12). However, in the absence of such occurrences, it is best to approach the situation with honesty and transparency. My recommended approach includes the following steps:

1. Reflect your observations to the individual, for example: 'It appears you have experienced circumstances that lead you to question God's goodness.'
2. Affirm the validity of their struggle or inquiry, such as: 'While I have not encountered that myself, I can appreciate why it would prompt doubts about God's goodness.'
3. Guide them toward appropriate resources or support, saying: 'I do not feel I am able to fully address your concerns, but I know someone with relevant experience who may be able to help.' If no referral is available, consider: 'I may need some time to reflect on your concerns; would you be open to meeting again for further discussion after I've given it some thought?'

The focus here is on identifying the reason and trying to positively deconstruct it. Positive deconstruction involves addressing barriers while intentionally reinforcing the underlying reasons for an individual's interest. For instance, do you remember Dave, whom I met at a coffee shop? Despite having undergone multiple brain-tumour surgeries, his barrier was unanswered prayer, and he sought hope amidst his physical and emotional struggles. By directing him to God who cares for our struggles and works against the adversary intent on harming us, Dave's curiosity deepened. I was able to guide his interest towards Jesus, and then present the decision he needed to make.

This pivotal moment signifies the culmination of dedicated efforts. As significant time and energy have been invested in prayer, building relationships, and sharing God's principles, individuals may reach a point where they consider making a commitment. Many have participated through sowing and nurturing, and now there is potential for making an eternal decision. Determining someone's readiness can be challenging; it ultimately becomes clear only when they are presented with the opportunity to commit their lives to Christ and respond accordingly. However, certain indicators – such as receptive attitudes during conversations about the gospel, positive body language, tone of voice, and affirming comments – may suggest openness.

It is important to tailor the message to the individual's needs, connecting relevant aspects of the gospel to their personal circumstances before extending an invitation to make a decision. A common approach might include stating: 'As discussed, Jesus died on the cross and rose again, paying the debt of our sin and defeating our enemy. He offers the gift of salvation, which encompasses forgiveness and the restoration of a relationship with him. This gift is to be received, not earned. Would you like to seek his forgiveness and commit to him as Lord and King?'

Usually someone ready just needs the gospel presented in a relevant and relatable way, and then a clarifying of the decision that needs to be made.

*

A point to note is that sometimes shifting someone from one position to another could take years. This is what we refer to as *cultivating* the harvest as opposed to *reaping* the harvest that is ready. Cultivating the harvest means building relationships through love, service, practical help, and prayer, while seeking God's guidance for opportunities to share your faith. It requires trusting God to provide moments for meaningful conversations that help others explore their beliefs.

On some occasions someone may seem like they are anti-God to begin with, but they are ready. Their reactions may seem hostile but that is the last strands of resistance before making a commitment.

So, while these scales can be very helpful to pinpoint where a person is at in their faith journey and therefore what to focus on, this is just a guide. Only God knows what is really going on in someone's heart.

In Acts 17, the apostle Paul was preaching the gospel to a crowd in Athens. It's interesting observing the three different types of responses to his message:

> *When they heard about the resurrection of the dead,* ***some of them sneered****, but others said, '****We want to hear you again*** *on this subject.' At that, Paul left the Council.* ***Some of the people became followers*** *of Paul and believed. Among them was Dionysius, a member of the Areopagus, also a woman named Damaris, and a number of others*
>
> Acts 17:32-34 (my emphasis)

Some believed and followed Paul, others became curious and wanted to hear more, and still more mocked and rejected the message. Going back to our prayer for open doors, here we see people with open hearts ready to respond. Imagine being there that day, hearing the apostle Paul, ministering the gospel with conviction and authority. When people responded, imagine his joy at their response. The Bible says that heaven rejoices when even just one sinner repents (Luke 15:7). There is a party in heaven! We get to rejoice with heaven when we share in a person's moment of repentance. God can and wants to use you to do the same.

Some doors are open to conversation, others are firmly closed and even hostile. Engaging with people who are unreceptive can be difficult, as I experienced when sharing the gospel at Imperial College with a group of atheists who openly ridiculed me. Proclaiming the gospel often requires courage and can come at personal cost, such as risking reputation or relationships. That's why abiding in Christ and knowing our identity in Him is essential; it anchors us against opposition and helps us remain loving, compassionate, patient and kind in the face of rejection.

Paul was faithful to share the good news. Their response, however, was between them and God. In the same way, let's be faithful to courageously and faithfully minister the gospel to the best of our ability and leave the results to God. You are more ready than you think!

CONCLUSION: SINCE IT'S NECESSARY, USE WORDS!

'KILL THE RUSSIANS!' was blazoned across his back, big and bold, with a graphic picture of a Ukrainian soldier holding a decapitated head. Trying to hide my shock, I gave him a smile and a friendly wave. He nodded in

acknowledgement. I could never have anticipated that five short days later, he would be hugging me tightly, tears streaming down his rounded cheeks, having just committed his life to Christ. We were strangers from vastly different worlds, speaking different languages, and from different generations. Yet somehow the gospel bridged the gap.

This happened during the war while on a ministry trip with my daughter. We were ministering at a youth camp and he was one of many who responded to the gospel in the packed camp-site meeting hall. A significant number of the youth expressed an interest in exploring the Christian faith for the first time because of what they heard and experienced.

Thanks to my dear friends, Kostya and Aya who invited me, this was the first time I was ministering the Gospel Steps (www.gospelsteps.com) in another language, and to youth – a test of simplicity, transferability and relatability. Most of the kids were not yet Christians. All of them had been impacted by the war; we heard first-hand how some were orphaned or had a lost parents and family members. Thankfully, by God's grace, lives were deeply impacted.

We had almost decided not to go. A few months prior, as the conflict escalated and drone and missile attacks became more frequent, safety was a serious consideration. After evaluating our options, we chose to proceed with the trip. Had we stayed, we would have lost this important opportunity to provide support and proclaim the gospel, which had a notable impact on the Ukrainian youth involved. We all need courage to overcome challenges in going. This applies whether it's a mission trip abroad, or reaching out to a neighbour.

At this point it is worth revisiting Romans 10:

> *How, then, can they call on the one they have not believed in? And how can they believe in the one of whom they have not heard? And how can they hear without someone preaching to them? And how can anyone preach unless they are sent? As it is written: 'How beautiful are the feet of those who bring good news!'*
>
> Romans 10:14-15

How will they know, unless we go? – it is necessary to use words. Clear communication is essential. Using SALT helps us assess where someone is in their faith journey so we can respond appropriately – whether by answering a question, listening, offering kindness, or praying for them.

Consider your own faith journey. Can you recognise times when you were far from God and then times when you became curious? Most likely it was not a journey that moved along the scale in one direction. There may have been times when you were anti-God and then moved to interest. Perhaps, something triggered you from being interested back to anti-God. Individuals you care about – whether they are loved ones for whom you are praying or strangers with whom you interact – will inevitably experience this kind of journey. Such a journey rarely progresses in a direct and consistent manner from -10 to 0.

Peter the great apostle, profoundly captures the heart of God towards those who are lost, in 2 Peter 3:9: *'The Lord is not slow in keeping his promise, as some understand*

slowness. Instead he is patient with you, not wanting anyone to perish, but everyone to come to repentance.'

It seems that God understands that all people are on a journey, and He does not give up on those not yet saved. Who are you praying for right now to come to faith? Can you identify clues that may help you identify if they are *Anti-God, Indifferent, Interested* or *Ready*? Pray into whatever you perceive. Ask the Holy Spirit to reveal what you are not yet seeing. Ask God for the courage and the wisdom you need for a meaningful conversation appropriate for where they are at. Before dismissing an opportunity, like we nearly did with our Ukraine mission, pray and ask God what He would like you to do.

*

What do you do when someone is ready and wants to commit their life to Christ? How we respond in that moment will impact what kind of follower of Jesus they become. Let's examine how best to help a new believer in their lifelong journey of being a follower of Jesus, a member of God's family and a citizen of His Kingdom.

YOUR NOTES

CHAPTER TWELVE

MULTIPLYING YOUR EVANGELISM FRUITFULNESS

They strained to see what he was pointing at. As their eyes adjusted to the darkness of the dimly-lit Chinese alley, they simultaneously heard and saw the slight rustle of the newspaper.

Then came the shock: babies left to die, abandoned there with no one to care for them! There wasn't just one, but several precious baby girls – innocent souls cast aside by a world that had failed to see their inherent worth.

This pivotal moment ignited a fire within the young couple, compelling them to leave the comforts of England and embark on a mission of love and redemption.

With unwavering determination, they established an orphanage ministry that would not only save countless lives, but eventually challenge and reshape government policies on orphan care.

We can learn from them. The need for a newborn baby to be nourished and cared for is obvious, but the need for spiritual newborns is less obvious, but no less essential. Just as infants require love, nourishment, and care to survive and thrive, so too do spiritual newborns need guidance and support.

The apostle Peter implores us in 1 Peter 2:2: *'Like newborn babies, crave pure spiritual milk, so that by it you may grow up in your salvation.'*

When an individual commits their life to Christ, they are reborn – fragile and dependent on the spiritual family around them. It is our sacred duty to provide the love, instruction, correction, and encouragement they need to mature in their faith and become a disciple of Christ.

Our call, as we pray, perceive and proclaim is to make, not just decisions for Christ, but to make disciples of Christ. Let's examine now what it means to be a disciple maker and the significant impact we can have through discipleship. We will also look at some practical guidelines for discipleship.

EMBRACING THE ROLE OF A SPIRITUAL MIDWIFE

When I was a student, Steven Curtis Chapman, a prominent global Christian artist, was coming to our city. Churches were recruited to help with follow up as he gathered the unsaved and proclaimed the gospel with impact. As a member of the follow up team, I recall being instructed that we were like spiritual midwives. What is a midwife? Someone who specialises in providing care for a mother and baby, before, during and after childbirth. In other words, we were given the responsibility, at this concert, to receive new spiritual babies into the world, provide the initial care until they were transitioned to their 'spiritual parents'.

We are called to be spiritual midwives – guiding new believers into the world of faith with tenderness and care. This role is not to be taken lightly; it is a divine responsibility that can shape the trajectory of a person's spiritual journey. When we lead someone to Christ, we must commit ourselves to ensure they are established in a loving, nurturing Christian community.

JESUS AS OUR EXAMPLE

In Matthew 4 Jesus started His earthly ministry by inviting a motley crew of fishermen, tax collectors and sinners on a journey of apprenticeship, to be His disciples. They bickered, they fought, they argued about who was the best. His final instruction to them, at the end of His earthly ministry was to go into all the world and make disciples (Matthew 28:19-20). In between He taught them, trained them, corrected them, modelled for them and empowered them to do as He had done. That motley crew of Jesus followers blazed a trail of gospel preaching, church planting and Kingdom advancement that turned the world upside down.

His ministry started and ended with discipleship. In between, He equipped and empowered them to keep doing what He did: make disciples! Evidently, His strategy to save the lost and advance His Kingdom worked and is still working.

THE CALL TO MULTIPLY: MAKE DISCIPLES NOT JUST DECISIONS

Aoife Keegan is an amazing leader I have the privilege of working with. She is the Europe Director for Every Nation Campus Ministries and a very fruitful disciple maker. She points out that if you are a super evangelist and lead one person to Christ every day then after twenty years you would have led 7300 people to Christ. Impressive. But for most of us, unattainable.

However, if you lead just one person to Christ every year, and disciple them to make disciple-making disciples, the results are initially not so impressive, but in the long run are staggering.

After five years you will have thirty-two disciple-making disciples compared to the super evangelist who would have reached 1825 people. But, after twenty years you will have 1,048,676 disciple-making disciples compared to the 7300 the super evangelist would have reached!

In the long run, the 'disciple-making disciples' approach is not only more attainable but also more impactful. I suspect this is the reason Jesus spent so much time withdrawing from crowds to spend time with His small group of future world-changers.

The inspiring story of Steve and Deborah Murrell's ministry in Manila serves as a testament to the exponential impact of effective discipleship. Through their commitment to making disciples rather than just decisions, they saw their church grow from a handful of students when they started in 1984, to over 50,000 members in 2011 when Steve published his book *WikiChurch* that gives an account of what happened. The ministry in Manila continues to multiply reaching tens of thousands in Manila and planting many disciple-making churches around the world as a result.

Part of their growth can be attributed to the 4Es discipleship process they developed. The 4Es is a straightforward and transferable discipleship framework that has been adopted by churches globally. The four core principles – Engage, Establish, Equip, and Empower – are designed to foster the development of disciple-making disciples. Discipleship begins with engaging individuals with the gospel. Once individuals respond, they are

established in the faith and integrated into Christian community. They are then equipped to serve effectively as ministers. Finally, they are empowered to reach others with the gospel. This cyclical process serves as a catalyst for multiplying discipleship efforts.

We must shift our focus from merely securing salvation decisions to cultivating mature reproducing disciples.

WHAT IS A DISCIPLE?

I am thankful to have heard Steve speak on discipleship many times. In his typical manner of providing clear, concise and compelling insights he offers a simple way of understanding Jesus' invitation to become a disciple of Jesus (a definition of what it means to be a disciple) based on Matthew 4:19, *'And He said to them, "Follow me, and I will make you fishers of men (people)"'*(ESV). We are called to be disciples and make disciples. A disciple of Jesus is someone who:

1. Follows Jesus.
2. Fellowships with other believers.
3. Fishes for men (people).

To put it simply, we follow Jesus in fellowship while fishing for the lost.

FOLLOW

Following Jesus means learning to be like Jesus. We do that through studying the Word of God and learning to obey His Word in all things. It's living the way of the Kingdom as modelled by Jesus and doing so through the help He provides.

FELLOWSHIP

You may wonder how we get the word *fellowship* from this text. Note that Jesus was speaking to more than one person. It says, *'And He said to them…'* Not singular but plural. Jesus' model of discipleship involved gathering a few into a relational journey where they grew into a missional community. They received instruction, correction, encouragement and opportunity to apply what they were learning.

FISH

Fishing for people is of course what we have been focusing on throughout this book. It involves having compassion for the lost and engaging them with the good news of God's Kingdom and His plan for salvation.

WHERE TO START WITH DISCIPLESHIP

What has helped you grow spiritually? Is there something that helped you that you can use to help others grow? Does your church have a follow-up and discipleship process? Is it biblical and Christ-centred? If yes, then start there. Use what your church or ministry uses. Why? You are establishing the new believer in the culture of their new Christian community. I am reluctant to provide prescriptive instruction for discipleship methods because

of how important it is to bring people into the culture of their new spiritual family.

If your church does not have discipleship resources, then why not consider doing a Bible study together reading through one of the gospels?

The Gospel of Mark is a good consideration as it is the shortest of the Gospels, focuses on who Jesus is, what He did, what He taught and has a strong emphasis on being a disciple. Focus on Jesus: study who He is, what He did, what He taught and how to grow to be like Him.

TIPS FOR ESTABLISHING NEW BELIEVERS

Here are some tips to help you be an effective spiritual midwife, to establish new believers in the faith after they've decided to follow Christ.

FOUNDATIONS

The first focus is biblical foundations. If possible, identify a discipleship tool designed for this. The Bible, when properly understood and applied is transformational, anchoring and life giving. Foundations are not just about gaining Bible knowledge but learning to obey because transformation only happens through application. (Matthew 28:20.) Not applying what we know is like a medical doctor knowing that smoking is destructive, but they still smoke.

RELATIONAL JOURNEY

- Keep the journey relational, not just instructional. When you journey relationally with someone, you foster trust. Through the trust that is established their hearts become more open to learn and apply what they learn. You also get to observe the destructive patterns in their lives that need freedom and repentance and have opportunity to minister to those areas.
- Establish them in Christian community as quickly as possible so that they can have multiple relational anchors for input and guidance.

TEACHING TO OBEY

- People tend to have more conviction about what they discover than what they are taught. When studying a text together, try ask questions about its meaning rather than just telling them the meaning.
- Transformation happens through application, not just information as previously stated. Help facilitate application. When they gain an insight, look for opportunity to turn that insight into a very practical, measurable commitment. e.g. 'I will pray for ten minutes at 6:30 a.m. every morning.' That is a better commitment than 'I will pray more.'
- Follow up on application commitments they make. Do not be harsh if they don't fulfil the commitment. Instead explore lovingly why they didn't and what they could do differently next time. Encourage them to not give up but to give it another go.

- Pray for them. Pray when you are with them, but also pray for them daily if you can for God to continue His work in them.
- Remember they are not your disciple; they are a disciple of Jesus. Always point them to Jesus, the one who loves them and instructs them.
- Do what you can but know your limitations. Philip the evangelist led an Ethiopian eunuch to Christ but was limited in the discipleship journey (Acts 8:26-40). We do what we can but leave the results to God.

FOCUS AND OUTCOMES

Whatever your method or preferred resource, it helps to have clear focus, and outcomes you are looking for. I have found the *5Fs of Spiritual Growth* very helpful.

1. FOUNDATIONS: Building a life rooted in obedience to God's Word.
2. FREEDOM: Embracing the liberating power of Christ's sacrifice.
3. FAITH: Developing unwavering trust in God's promises.
4. FAMILY: Fostering loving relationships within Christian community.
5. FRUITFULNESS: Bearing the fruit of the Spirit and fulfilling God's unique calling.

These are guidelines for your focus but remember the results are produced through what God does in their lives. Through the relational journey of discipleship, we facilitate God working in their lives through His Word, through the Holy Spirit and through Christian community.

CONCLUSION: GENERATIONAL MULTIPLICATION

In conclusion, those who respond to the gospel need nurture. Spiritual maturity happens in spiritual family. As spiritual midwives, we have a glorious opportunity to do what we can to help a new believer go on to spiritual maturity.

> John, one of Jesus' disciples, provides significant insights. *'I am writing to you,* ***dear children,*** *because your sins have been forgiven on account of his name. I am writing to you,* ***fathers,*** *because you know him who is from the beginning. I am writing to you,* ***young men,*** *because you have overcome the evil one'*
>
> 1 John 2:12-13 (my emphasis)

It is noteworthy that John addresses children, young men, and fathers, symbolising different stages of spiritual development. Children are expected to grow in maturity, eventually reaching a stage where they can guide others as fathers do. This journey begins with the forgiveness of sins, progresses through overcoming the evil one (God's enemy), and culminates in a deeper relationship with God (abiding). Sustainable spiritual growth should move believers beyond initial struggles with sin toward a life marked by victory, holiness, and closer unity with the Father.

Additionally, there is an implicit emphasis on multiplication within the faith community. The progression from child to father implies the responsibility of fostering new believers through prayer, discernment of opportunities, and effective communication of the gospel message – pray, perceive, proclaim! The ultimate objective is not merely to nurture spiritual children, but to encourage their growth into spiritual parents, grandparents, and beyond, ensuring continued generational multiplication within the faith. The apostle Paul modelled and instructed this as a spiritual father in his letter to his spiritual son, Timothy:

'And the things you have heard me say in the presence of many witnesses entrust to reliable people who will also be qualified to teach others' (2 Timothy 2:2).

Paul taught Timothy to teach others to also teach others, ensuring generational multiplication. Steve Murrell offers a warning worth noting, he says that we are just one generation away from extinction, referring to the need to reach the lost, establish new believers and raise leaders.[1] If we only 'follow' Jesus while enjoying 'fellowship' with believers without 'fishing', we risk extinction and breaking the generational chain that goes all the way back to the first disciples that followed Jesus.

*

As we have looked at raising our readiness through cultivating our willingness, we've also clarified the powerful, life-transforming, world-changing message, now it is time to put on the shoes of readiness and go!

Remember, when you go, you don't go alone. You are joining Jesus on a journey of adventure to seek and save the lost. You don't need to go in your own strength. The work of salvation is a supernatural, divinely-orchestrated, Spirit-empowered Kingdom work to participate in.

We will conclude by exploring how we rely on God's strength beyond our own as we prepare ourselves and go to the harvest.

MORE READY THAN YOU THINK

Martin Luther King, Jr is believed to have said, 'Faith is taking the first step, even when you don't see the whole staircase.'[1]

If you haven't already, then it is time to put on your shoes of readiness and step into your calling as a witness for Christ. It may be your first courageous step into the unknown, but as Luther King exhorted, you don't need to see the outcomes or have guaranteed results before you begin the journey.

It is natural to want to feel fully ready before we go because we think this will guarantee success. But there is always risk in going – there's a possibility of failure and rejection – but if we wait, we stagnate. In going, we grow, but it does require boldness and courage.

While touring Europe following his presidency, Theodore Roosevelt delivered a speech at the Sorbonne on the 23rd April 1910, titled: '*Citizenship in a Republic*'. Here is a stirring portion that challenges us to step out despite the very real possibility of failure:

> It is not the critic who counts; not the man who points out how the strong man stumbles, or where the doer of deeds could have done them better. The credit belongs to the man who is actually in the arena, whose face is marred by dust and sweat and blood; who strives valiantly; who errs, who comes short again and again...

> who at the best knows in the end the triumph of high achievement, and who at the worst, if he fails, at least fails while daring greatly.[2]

It is time to dare greatly.

Remember the shoeshine guy? What started as a reluctant travel-weary conversation about getting my brand-new trainers polished, ended in Mr Bag Polisher making a life-transforming decision to follow Jesus.

At the start of this book, I invited you to join me in putting on your shoes of readiness, cultivating your willingness and raising your readiness. I encouraged you to join Jesus in the adventurous journey of getting the good news of the gospel where it needs to go and getting it there on time. I appealed for us to avoid missing opportunities like I did with Trevor and instead experience many shoeshine guy encounters!

Maybe you have already stepped out and started the journey of praying, perceiving and even proclaiming the good news of the gospel. You may have had some SALT conversations and discovered a few open doors as you've ministered, and perhaps you have had the incredible joy of leading someone to follow Christ. But possibly some of you might still not be feeling quite ready enough. What do you do if this is you? Firstly, I have good news: you are more ready than you think.

Perhaps the point below will be helpful to you.

COMPETENCE NEEDS TO BE RECEIVED

There is still one final factor to consider: your competence. Where does your competence come from? One would

most likely think that competence comes from being trained. And in most cases, it does. However, when it comes to ministering the gospel, there is a dimension of competence that comes not through training, but through *receiving.*

I am excited to share this one vital and final game-changing insight, which makes all the difference in raising your readiness.

> *Not that we are **competent in ourselves** to claim anything for ourselves, but our **competence comes from God**. He has made us **competent as ministers** of a new covenant—not of the letter but of the Spirit; for the letter kills, but the **Spirit gives life**.*
>
> 2 Corinthians 3:5-6 (my emphasis)

You are a minister of the New Covenant in Jesus. The New Covenant Paul is talking about, is the gospel. It is the means for restoring our wonderful, but broken world and our wonderful, but broken lives; it is the good news we get to proclaim.

The gap between your competency and your responsibility is filled with His sufficiency. Your competence as a minister of this covenant comes from God. Wow! Did you get that? Your competence, when it comes to sharing your faith, is something you receive. But how?

MADE TO FISH WITH POWER

Do you remember what Jesus, the carpenter, said He would make you into? He said, if you follow Him, He'd make you a fisher of people. You may recall I used the analogy of a toaster and a kettle being used according to their purpose. You'll destroy a toaster if you use it to boil water. But if you want toast, it contributes wonderfully! That's why it's important to know what you are made for and to function in your design. You are made to be Christ's witness in this world and to proclaim the good news of His Kingdom.

However, a toaster without power will not make toast. Just like an electrical appliance needs power to fulfil its potential, you need God's power and His supernatural ability to fulfil yours. Before Jesus fulfilled His earthly ministry, and before He passed the baton to His trained and willing disciples, He gave them this one last final promise, referring to what they would experience at Pentecost:

> *But you will receive power when the Holy Spirit comes on you; and you will be my witnesses in Jerusalem, and in all Judea and Samaria, and to the ends of the earth. After he said this, he was taken up before their very eyes, and a cloud hid him from their sight*
>
> Acts 1:8-9

Just pause and think about that for a moment. They were trained and willing. They had the potential but were not quite ready. There was one last instruction and promise Jesus left them: to receive the Holy Spirit and as a result, the power to be witnesses.

This book is titled, *More Ready Than You Think*. Remember, our readiness is not dependent on us only, because you and I do not have the ability to save anyone. Salvation is a work of the Holy Spirit who convicts hearts of their desperate state of sinfulness and who bears witness to the truth. God is the one who enables a person to be born again of His Spirit, making them a member of His family and a citizen of His Kingdom. But God has chosen to use us, in partnership with Him, to be bearers of the good news of the gospel.

While you and I are designed and made to be His witnesses, we need His power to function.

POWERLESS FOLLOWERS UNLEASHED WITH POWER

It is remarkable that within just a few short weeks, after witnessing Jesus' mutilated body hanging on a splintered Roman cross, the disciples were unleashed with boldness, proclaiming the good news of Jesus on the very streets that had seen Him carrying His cross. Those disciples knew that they risked the same thing, and some did, eventually suffering similar torturous deaths.

How did they find the courage, the boldness, and the competence to proclaim Jesus to the same people who put Him on the cross? They did so through the promised power received when the Holy Spirit came upon them at Pentecost. The same Holy Spirit promised to them then, is promised to us now. Jesus said that you will receive the power to be His witnesses, and go *'...to the ends of the earth.'* We are still called to take the gospel to the ends of the earth, starting with our neighbours, and like the disciples, we need the Holy Spirit's power for boldness and supernatural abilities.

How wonderful that Jesus doesn't just send us! He invites us to join Him on the journey of His mission, filled with the Holy Spirit, and functioning in His power.

Here are just some of the benefits, briefly explained, of functioning in the power of the Holy Spirit.

BENEFITS OF THE POWER

- **Directed to the harvest**: you have the Spirit of God living inside of you who can direct you to the ripe harvest. He knows the harvest better than you do! After all, our senses and perceptions can deceive us.
- **Enemy defeated**: greater is His Spirit in you than the spirit that is in the world (1 John 4:4).
- **Courage and boldness**: The Holy Spirit gives courage and boldness (2 Timothy 1:7).
- **Supernatural ability**: The Holy Spirit can enable you to share your faith with supernatural gifts such as healings, miracles and knowledge (1 Corinthians 12:1-11).

God by His grace, can use you if you are willing, but much more significantly when you are plugged into His power and operating with His abilities flowing in and through you. Start by abiding and spending time in God's presence. Learn to listen to God's guidance and invite the Holy Spirit to minister through you. Then, be willing to take the risk and offer to pray for people. Either respond to a need you perceive or ask them for a need you can pray for. It can be scary, and there will be times when nothing happens. That's okay. Focus on being faithful, not fruitful. Fruitfulness will come with faithfulness.

I was doing an outreach on a university in the Netherlands, and had an opportunity for a deep conversation with a curious atheist. After presenting evidence for God from science, philosophy and history, I explained to her that miracles and healings are also evidence for God, and because she had a pair of crutches by her side I asked if I could pray for her healing. To be honest I expected her to say no, but she was willing. After I prayed, do you have any idea what happened? Nothing. So, I asked if I could pray again. Still nothing. I didn't get flustered or apologetic about it. I knew that my heart was filled with compassion, my trust was in God, and I had done what God wanted me to do. So, I explained to her that sometimes prayers are not answered right away. I urged her that if she suddenly experienced a supernatural healing, then to honour the God who loved her enough to do that for her. She nodded and said she would.

As it turned out, some of our team later had a conversation with the same girl and remarkably she told them she was an agnostic, not an atheist – her confession had changed! They ended up praying with her to accept Jesus as her Lord and Saviour. I am persuaded that the conversation we had, and my praying for her, contributed to raising her readiness to later respond to the gospel.

In contrast, my friend Roshni also prayed for a student on crutches, at the University of Cape Town. On this occasion the student described a warmth flowing through her injured ankle and she was instantly healed. She jumped up and down and ran around the quad! Roshni shared the gospel with her and her friend, and both made commitments to follow Jesus. That same night Roshni saw another student, and this time received a picture that she knew was a message from God for her. She went and introduced herself, told this girl that she was a Christian and asked if she could share the message God had given her. The girl said yes. When Roshni shared the picture, the girl burst into tears and once again Roshni led this girl and her friend to Jesus.

On another occasion I was the guest speaker at a church in Namibia, and a church member had been visiting a young man in the cancer ward of a hospital nearby. She asked if I could pray for him. He had a tumour the size of a tennis ball on the back of his leg. The first time I prayed nothing happened. So, we prayed again and suddenly his body began to shake as he burst into tears. He said that like a deflating balloon, the tumour completely disappeared under his hand!

I can share many stories when nothing happened, but likewise there are many instances when God did do something amazing in response to prayer. Whether the person is healed or not, they are assured that they are loved, that I care and have compassion for their struggle, and that God does too. This is my focus.

Without risk, there is no reward. Better to be the man in the arena, than the spectator who knows neither triumph nor defeat.

*

As we come to the end of this book, we are approaching the beginning of a lifelong, exhilarating journey, wearing shoes of readiness, empowered by the Holy Spirit for leading many to Christ. God does not send you out; He

invites you in. He is already in the harvest; you are joining Him in His divine plans and purposes to seek and save the lost. He has good works prepared beforehand for you to walk in. Jesus said to pray to the Lord of the harvest for more labourers; you are ready to be an answer to that prayer. Perhaps you are even more ready than you think!

Before you pause and pray and open your heart to receive the promised provision for being a witness, here's a closing thought from 2 Chronicles 16:9. *'For the eyes of the Lord run to and fro throughout the whole earth, to show Himself strong on behalf of those whose heart is loyal to Him' (NKJV).*

Remember, there is a competency we can receive (2 Corinthians 3:5-6). God is looking for hearts ready to receive the competency He can give. He is looking; give Him a moment now for Him to find you, to show Himself strong on your behalf.

PAUSE AND PRAY

Pause and pray right now. Close your eyes and give God your fullest attention. Let go of every distracting thought. Choose to believe and receive the promise of the Holy Spirit and the power He provides for you to be His witness. Take a moment now to receive as you pray, with faith for what Jesus promised:

'Holy Spirit, I welcome you. Fill me now. Empower me. I receive you.'

Pause and receive.

Sometimes, we receive by faith, not by sight or feelings. Our trust is in a good loving Father who hears us when we pray. He is a loving Father who knows how to give good gifts to His children (Luke 11:11-13).

Now, it's time to step into the arena. You are more ready than you think!

APPENDIX: RESOURCES FOR RAISING YOUR READINESS

MOREREADYTHANYOUTHINK.COM

Personal growth is an ongoing process, and readiness can be intentionally developed. At morereadythanyouthink.com, our mission is to equip, empower, and mobilise individuals to share the gospel effectively. We are committed to continually exploring innovative approaches to support this goal. Updates regarding newly developed resources will be posted on the website to assist in enhancing your readiness. We invite you to visit the website to discover opportunities that may enrich your journey in sharing the gospel.

GET EQUIPPED IN CONVERSATION EVANGELISM

Engage Training is a course to equip confidence and competence to share your faith. Developed by Frans and Deb Olivier and launched in 2018, it has equipped and empowered many across several continents and many nations. The principles, many of which have been inspired and motivated in this book, are simple and transferrable to any culture which was the intent when we designed the course.

- Online Engage Training is a live, interactive evangelism course, currently offered twice yearly with plans for an 'on-demand' version.
- We feature experiences from others, host group discussions, hold Q&A sessions and more.
- The course includes a comprehensive manual containing eight chapters.
- The online training spans four weeks, covering two chapters weekly, with optional gospel coaching.
- In every course conducted, some participants have indicated that they led others to Christ prior to finishing the training.

To get details for how you could do Engage Training or receive updates on new developments use the QR code below.

ONLINE DIGITAL GOSPEL TRACT: GOSPELSTEPS.COM

What is gospelsteps.com? This is an online digital tract designed for versatile applications. After engaging in a discussion about the gospel, you may refer individuals to the website for further exploration of its message. It's a safe space where only the gospel is presented and free from information on equipping or resourcing believers. If you've led someone to Christ, this can help them review and deepen their understanding of the gospel, and provide assurance of salvation. It can be used to engage in regular Bible study with individuals interested in learning about the faith, utilizing the provided Bible verses.

Please note that most modern web browsers now offer a feature for translating websites into various languages. When sharing the online digital tract with individuals whose first language is not English, you may encourage them to utilise this function to read the material in their preferred language.

GOSPEL STEPS RESOURCES: GOSPELSTEPS.STORE

The gospel seed needs scattering not just planting. To get equipped for scattering the gospel, we have merch that's made to scatter. To order wristbands, wallet cards or other merch we develop, use the QR code below.

YOUR NOTES

ACKNOWLEDGEMENTS

Many individuals have accompanied me throughout this journey – some have contributed to my personal growth and preparedness, while others have exemplified remarkable commitment. Each of you has inspired me, whether you are aware of it or not, and I am deeply grateful, though there are too many to name individually.

I would like to extend special recognition to my exceptional editor and writing coach, Jenni Pretorius (née Hill – jennhill.edits@gmail.com). Our collaboration began with mission work in China in the early 2000s, continuing more recently with the development of this book. Jenni dedicated endless hours to reading and revising the manuscript, providing patient guidance as I honed my writing skills. Her insight – often surpassing her considerable expertise – helped fill gaps, restructure, and refine the content, ensuring that the message resonates profoundly. I am sincerely appreciative of Jenni's invaluable contribution; this book would not be what it is without her.

I hope this book has encouraged your prayer life. Every believer benefits from a dedicated prayer partner – our family is grateful for Ruth Cairns, whom we met during missions in Europe and China in the late 1990s. Thank you, Ruth, for your unwavering prayer support; its impact will only be fully revealed in eternity.

I am also grateful for the outstanding colleagues I have the opportunity to work with. Jenna McGuinness, a prominent church-based evangelist and a member of the leadership team for Every Nation Europe Evangelism, serves as an exemplary role model – not only in leading individuals to Christ but also in equipping others to do likewise.

Thanks to my exceptional Executive Assistant, Anna Kruger – for your unwavering dedication and willingness to take on any challenge, even unfamiliar ones. I appreciate all you have done to help complete this book.

Finally, thanks to Rona Miller and Themba Malaba for the significant feedback and input you gave, especially for triggering what made Section 2 what it is. You gave me a lot more work to do, but I forgive you and thank you.

ENDNOTES

Preface

1. https://youtube.com/shorts/1gTMrh7YwzA?si=PjwAVCbWjWMdKTRh

Introduction

1. https://home.snu.edu/~hculbert/intime.htm?utm_source=perplexity

Chapter one: Raising Your Readiness

1. https://tfl.gov.uk/info-for/media/press-releases/2023/november/latest-tfl-figures-show-the-tube- reaching-4-million-journeys-per-day?t&utm_source=perplexity

Chapter three: Willingness from Being

1. William Rice Broocks, *The Gift of the Evangelist* (Dissertation for Fuller Seminary 2010; School of Intercultural Studies), p. 27.
2. Ibid.,p.39

Chapter four: Willingness from Compassion

1. *The Greater Good Science Center Magazine* (2025) What is Compassion?

2. John Maxwell, *Everyone Communicates Few Connect: What the Most Effective People Do Differently* (Thomas Nelson, 2010), p. 4.

Chapter six: The Magnificence of God

1. Blaise Pascal, *Pensées* (London: Penguin Classics, 1995)

Chapter seven: The Meaning of Sin

1. C.S. Lewis, *Mere Christianity (*Harper Collins, 2011), p. 38.
2. http://news.bbc.co.uk/1/hi/sci/tech/557605.stm?utm_source=perplexity R.A. Grimes, (2001). *Malicious Mobile Code: Virus Protection for Windows.* O'Reilly. Section 5.7.
3. A. Greenberg, The Confessions of Marcus Hutchins, the Hacker Who Saved the Internet (2020, May 12)

Chapter eight: The Magnitude of Restoration

1. Online article: https://rebatirnotredamedeparis.fr/en/mecenes
2. Dallas Willard. *Life Without Lack: Living in the Fullness of Psalm 23* (Nashville: Thomas Nelson, 2018)

Chapter nine: Pray–Cultivating God-dependency

1. R.Bonnke, *Evangelism by Fire: Keys for Effectively Reaching Others with the Gospel* (Charisma House, 2011), chapter 20
2. *Spurgeon's Sermons Volume 12: 1866*

3. Wayne Sandeman, *Revival Rain,* (Every Nation Durban, 2022), *p. Xii.*
4. Ibid., p. 3.
5. Ibid., p. 4.

Chapter ten: Perceive–the Power of Perceiving People

1. Cheryl A. Elton *Kingdom Faith Ministries International. Living in the Miraculous: Smith Wigglesworth Part 1* (Saturday, May 6 2023)
2. Merriam-Webster.com
3. https://www.oxfordreference.com/display/10.1093/acref/9780199657681.001.0001/acref-9780199657681-e-6229
4. Kenneth E. Bailey, *Jesus Through Middle Eastern Eyes* (SPCK, 2008), p. 170-185.

Chapter eleven: Proclaim: A Simple Strategy

1. *Preach the Gospel, and Since It's Necessary, Use Words:* Tabletalk magazine (Ligonier Ministries) June 1, 2012 Online on the Ligonier Ministries site
2. Nick Pollard, *Evangelism Made Slightly Less Difficult: How to Interest People Who Aren't Interested.* (Leicester: InterVarsity Press , 1997)

Chapter twelve: Multiplying your Evangelism Fruitfulness

1. https://www.google.com/url?q=https: //place.asburyseminary.edu/cgi/viewcontent.cgi?article%3D2431%26context%3Decommonsatsdissertations%26utm_source%3

Dperplexity&source=gmail-imap&ust=1752650412000000&usg=AOvVaw1zUmIWmpfmi_ewkhkLG31J

Conclusion

1. King, Jr. Research and Education Institute. (n.d.). Frequently requested quotations. Stanford University. Retrieved August 16, 2025, from https://kinginstitute.stanford.edu/king-resources/frequently-requested-quotations
2. T. Roosevelt, (1910, April 23). Citizenship in a Republic [Speech delivered at the Sorbonne, Paris]. The American Presidency Project. https://www.presidency.ucsb.edu/documents/address-the-sorbonne-paris-france-citizenship-republic.

YOUR NOTES